Prehistoric Culture Change on Southern Vancouver Island

The applicability of current explanations of the Marpole Transition

Terence Clark

BAR International Series 2745
2015

Published in 2016 by
BAR Publishing, Oxford

BAR International Series 2745

Prehistoric Culture Change on Southern Vancouver Island

ISBN 978 1 4073 1404 4

© T Clark and the Publisher 2015

The author's moral rights under the 1988 UK Copyright,
Designs and Patents Act are hereby expressly asserted.

All rights reserved. No part of this work may be copied, reproduced, stored,
sold, distributed, scanned, saved in any form of digital format or transmitted
in any form digitally, without the written permission of the Publisher.

BAR Publishing is the trading name of British Archaeological Reports (Oxford) Ltd.
British Archaeological Reports was first incorporated in 1974 to publish the BAR
Series, International and British. In 1992 Hadrian Books Ltd became part of the BAR
group. This volume was originally published by Archaeopress in conjunction with
British Archaeological Reports (Oxford) Ltd / Hadrian Books Ltd, the Series principal
publisher, in 2015. This present volume is published by BAR Publishing, 2016.

Printed in England

PUBLISHING

BAR titles are available from:

	BAR Publishing
	122 Banbury Rd, Oxford, OX2 7BP, UK
EMAIL	info@barpublishing.com
PHONE	+44 (0)1865 310431
FAX	+44 (0)1865 316916
	www.barpublishing.com

ABSTRACT

This thesis presents the results of research on the transition from Locarno Beach archaeological culture type (3500/3300 -2500/2400 BP) to Marpole culture type (2500/2400 -1500/1100 BP) within the Gulf of Georgia region of the Northwest Coast. Nearly 6000 artifacts from seven Southern Vancouver Island archaeological sites were typologically reclassified and added to previously recorded data from twenty Gulf of Georgia site components. Following the methods of Matson et al. (1980) and Burley (1980), multidimensional scaling was used to examine variability within the Marpole culture type. Results show the continuation of the Old Musqueam, Beach Grove and Garrison subphases of Marpole and the addition of a fourth named Bowker Creek.

Based on spatial and temporal distribution, I have re-interpreted the culture historical sequence and assigned both the Old Musqueam and Bowker Creek subphases to the Locarno Beach culture type, thus changing the date of the Locarno Beach – Marpole transition to around 2000 BP. My results show that Southern Vancouver Island may exhibit a different culture history than the Fraser River. I also offer an explanation of this transition and insight on the rise of sociocultural complexity in the Gulf of Georgia.

TABLE OF CONTENTS

Abstract i
Table of Contents ii
List of Figures iii
List of Tables iii
Acknowledgments iv

CHAPTER 1. INTRODUCTION 1

CHAPTER 2. DISCUSSION OF CURRENT KNOWLEDGE 3
2.1. Units of Analysis- Typology, Phases and Culture Types 3
2.2. The Regional Sequence- Locarno Beach; *technology, subsistence, settlement, sites, dating.* Marpole; *technology, subsistence, settlement, sites, dating, Subphases* 6

CHAPTER THREE. EXPLANATIONS OF PREHISTORIC CULTURE CHANGE 18
3.1 Discontinuity Explanations 18
3.2 Continuity Explanations 21

CHAPTER FOUR. SOUTHERN VANCOUVER ISLAND AND EXPLANATIONS OF 26
4.1. Culture Change 26
4.2. The Working Hypotheses 27

CHAPTER FIVE. DATA SET AND ANALYSIS 29
5.1. Sites, Artifacts, Analysis, Southern Vancouver Island 29

CHAPTER SIX. RESULTS 42
6.1. Dimensions One and Two, Dimensions Three and Four 43-48

CHAPTER SEVEN. INTERPRETATION 49
7.1. Regional Culture Historical Sequence, The Working Hypotheses 49-54
7.2. Explanations of Prehistoric Culture Change 54-58

CHAPTER EIGHT. CONCLUSION 59

REFERENCES CITED 60

APPENDIX ONE: RADIOCARBON DATING 68

APPENDIX TWO: ARTIFACT FREQUENCIES 73

APPENDIX THREE: DISTANCE MATRIX 82

APPENDIX FOUR: FACTOR MATRIX 84

LIST OF TABLES

Table 2.1	Locarno Beach Culture Type Diagnostic Traits	6-7
Table 2.2	Archaeological Sites with a Known Locarno Beach Component	9
Table 2.3	Marpole Culture Type Diagnostic Traits	9-10
Table 2.4	Archaeological Sites with a Known Marpole Component	10
Table 2.5	Subphases of Marpole Site Components	12
Table 3.1	Continuity Explanations	22
Table 5.1	Description of Southern Vancouver Island Sites	30-32
Table 5.2	Radiocarbon Age Estimates for Southern Vancouver Island Sites	31
Table 5.3	Description of Artifacts	32-33, 38
Table 6.1	Cluster Composition	45
Table A1.1	Radiocarbon Age Estimates for Selected Gulf of Georgia Site Components	71-72
Table A2.1	Artifact Frequencies	73-81
Table A3.1	Distance Matrix	82-83
Table A4.1	Factor Matrix	84-85

LIST OF FIGURES

Figure 2.1	Gulf of Georgia Regional Culture History	3
Figure 2.2	Economic Plateaus Explanation of Gulf of Georgia Culture Change	5
Figure 2.3	Map of Locarno Beach Culture Type Components	8
Figure 2.4	Map of Marpole Culture Type Components	11
Figure 2.5	Dimensions 1 and 2 of Metric Multidimensional Scaling: Results of 20 Marpole Components	13
Figure 2.6	Ward's Cluster Analysis of Dimensions 1 and 2 of Metric Multidimensional Scaling Results of 20 Marpole Components	14
Figure 2.7	Dimension 3 and 4 of Metric Multidimensional Scaling: Results of 20 Marpole Components	15
Figure 2.8	Map of Marpole Subphase Components	16
Figure 3.1	Development of the Gulf of Georgia Variant of the Northwest Coast Cultural Pattern	19
Figure 3.2	Deviation-Amplifying Model of the Evolution of Status Inequality, The Northwest Coast Example	24
Figure 5.1	Map of Southern Vancouver Island Study Area, DcRt and DcRu	30
Figure 5.2	Artifacts of Chipped Stone	34
Figure 5.3	Artifacts of Ground and Pecked Stone	35
Figure 5.4	Artifacts of Bone	36
Figure 5.5	Artifacts of Antler and Shell	37
Figure 5.6	Distance Matrix and Multidimensional Scaling between 10 U.S. Cities	39
Figure 5.7	City Block Distance versus Euclidean Distance	40
Figure 6.1	Dimensions 1 and 2 of Metric Multidimensional Scaling: Results of 27 Marpole Components	43
Figure 6.2	Map of Gulf of Georgia Locarno Beach and Marpole Components by Subphase	44
Figure 6.3	Ward's Cluster Analysis of Dimensions 1 and 2 of Metric Multidimensional Scaling: Results of 27 Marpole Components	46
Figure 6.4	Dimensions 3 and 4 of Metric Multidimensional Scaling: Results of 27 Marpole Components	47
Figure 7.1	Currently Accepted Regional Culture Historical Sequence	49
Figure 7.2	Raw Radiocarbon Age Estimates for Selected Gulf of Georgia Site Components	52
Figure 7.3	Newly Proposed Regional Culture Historical Sequence	53
Figure A1.1	Radiocarbon Dating Calibration Curve	69

ACKNOWLEDGMENTS

This monograph is based on my M.A. thesis from the University of Victoria, Victoria, British Columbia, Canada. It is slightly modified from its original state. I would like to take this opportunity to thanks some of the many people that helped this thesis come this far. First and foremost is my supervisor, Dr. Quentin Mackie. His support of this research was invaluable. I would also like to thank the remaining members of my examination committee: Dr. Nicholas Roland, Dr. Steve Acheson, Dr. John Lutz and Dr. Gay Frederick. I am also deeply indebted to several archaeologists who provided assistance. Dr. R.G. Matson allowed me access to his data, his computer program and helped me throughout the statistical progress of this thesis. He was consistently available for my questions and concerns and I thank him for that.

Dr. Donald Mitchell proved to be an important sounding board for my ideas and an invaluable reference in Northwest Coast archaeology. Nancy Romaine of the Royal British Columbia Museum allowed me access to the artifacts from Southern Vancouver Island that were reclassified in this thesis. She also helped sort out the archaeological components from DcRt 15. Becky Wigen helped shape my ideas of prehistoric culture change. Dr. Leland Donald answered many of my statistical questions. I am also indebted to Joanne Cumberland for her editorial advice Baillie Card for formatting assistance.

I would also like to thank my family and friends, without whom I would not have been able to finish.

This monograph is dedicated to my father, Gordon Clark, my biggest supporter, who taught me about perseverance and the importance of each day.

CHAPTER 1. INTRODUCTION

This thesis examines an important but somewhat ambiguous period of Northwest Coast prehistory. The Marpole culture type, although not completely understood, is one of the most important time periods, anthropologically, for the central Northwest Coast culture area. It is believed that Marpole gave rise to important markers of cultural complexity not commonly seen in foraging groups. While the thesis question "Can the shift from Locarno Beach to Marpole on Southern Vancouver Island be explained in terms of the existing culture historical framework?", examines a particular geographic and temporal case, larger anthropological questions are also looked at. As Marpole marks the rise of status inequality and sociocultural complexity, the study of Marpole is a crucible for the study of the larger anthropological question of the development of sociocultural complexity.

Marpole has been the focus of a century-long debate regarding population movement on the South Coast of British Columbia. Differences in artifact assemblages between Marpole and the preceding Locarno Beach culture type have led many archaeologists to invoke a population replacement as an explanation for the rise of Marpole. Currently, a more widely accepted view of Marpole as an *in situ* development predominates in the field of Northwest Coast archaeology yet the population replacement explanation still exists. This thesis offers new data to advance this longstanding debate.

The regional culture historical sequence depicts Marpole as a culture type existing between 2500/2400 and 1500/1100 years before present or BP. This thesis looks at the validity of that assignment and questions whether Marpole is a truly regional phenomenon. The Marpole culture type, although well defined in the literature, is not well known on Southern Vancouver Island. This study examines Southern Vancouver Island in relation to the culture historical sequence during the Marpole transition to examine the applicability of the culture history region-wide.

This thesis draws heavily on the work of Matson et al. (1980) and is essentially a replication of that study with additional new data from Southern Vancouver Island. The Matson et al. (1980) study used metric multidimensional scaling of twenty archaeological site components from the Gulf of Georgia region to examine variability within the Marpole culture type. Similar multidimensional scaling has been done for this thesis with seven new Southern Vancouver Island site components added to the original data from Matson et al. (1980). The results shed more light on the geographic and temporal variation within the Marpole culture type and offer some clues as to the rise of sociocultural complexity.

These next two chapters present the relevant background information for this study and pose the problem this thesis sets out to address.

The second chapter serves to acquaint the reader with the current state of knowledge of Northwest Coast archaeology. Chapter Two looks at all of the pertinent definitions required for this thesis and discusses the historical development of these terms. The typology, the culture types and the regional culture historical sequence are all defined and explained. These definitions will be used throughout the remainder of this thesis.

Chapter Three looks at existing explanations of the Locarno Beach to Marpole transition for the entire Gulf of Georgia region. Differing theories are weighed against current evidence to explain culture change at that time. The debate over dislocation versus continuity is examined and evaluated using the current state of Northwest Coast archaeological knowledge.

Chapter Four briefly outlines the fit of Southern Vancouver Island to the Gulf of Georgia explanations of culture change. Within this chapter the validity of region-wide explanations of the Locarno Beach to Marpole transition are questioned. Arising from this discussion a thesis question is proposed and defended. Three working hypotheses are presented as possible answers to the thesis question.

Chapters Five, Six and Seven look at analysis and results related to the thesis problem presented in first half of the thesis. They discuss the process of answering the thesis question from data collection and analysis to results and interpretation.

The fifth chapter outlines the data set and analytical procedures to be used in this study. The quality and nature of the data are examined. The archaeological sites included, and artifact typology utilized in this thesis, are reviewed. In addition a discussion of the statistical procedures employed in this thesis and how they have been used to answer the thesis question follows.

Chapter Six presents the results of multidimensional scaling and cluster analysis. The patterns discovered show the continuation of the Old Musqueam, Beach Grove and Garrison subphases and the addition of a fourth subphase named Bowker Creek. The nature of the new Bowker Creek subphase then becomes central to interpretations presented in Chapter Seven. The working hypotheses are examined and the thesis question is answered.

Following this, Chapter Seven re-examines the regional culture historical sequence from Chapter Two and the explanations of culture change from Chapter Three. The question of the applicability of the culture historical sequence region-wide is addressed. In light of my findings, a revised regional culture historical sequence is presented. The dislocation versus continuity debate is revisited with addition of the thesis data. I also take this opportunity to offer my own explanation of culture change across the Locarno Beach - Marpole transition.

The concluding chapter orients my results within the larger scope of Northwest Coast archaeology and suggests future avenues of inquiry.

CHAPTER 2. DISCUSSION OF CURRENT KNOWLEDGE

This chapter lays the background for a great deal of this thesis. It discusses the state of current knowledge regarding the culture historical sequence, the culture types and the regional artifact typology. Following this discussion, Chapter Three examines some of the explanations of culture change related to the regional culture history and the culture types presented here.

The Regional Sequence
The Gulf of Georgia region has been subject to archaeological inquiry for over 100 years. During that time numerous attempts to reconstruct local culture historical events have been made. Borden (1950, 1951), Carlson (1960) and King (1950) have developed local sequences.

Since Donald Mitchell (1971b) unified several of these local sequences into a broader regional culture historical sequence for the entire Gulf of Georgia region, the Gulf has been seen as a homogeneous unit of analysis. This has been a positive step in the greater understanding of Northwest Coast prehistory, however it has also served to gloss over variation within the Gulf of Georgia region.

The currently accepted culture historical sequence has five archaeological units dating from the initial colonization of the region to the coming of Europeans. Figure 2.1, shows the Gulf of Georgia sequence. This thesis deals primarily with the Locarno Beach and Marpole units of the sequence.

Locarno Beach and Marpole have been described alternately as phases and as culture types. The distinction between phase and culture type and the definition of each is not always straightforward. The definition of phase that many Northwest Coast archaeologists use (Burley 1980, Abbott 1972) comes from Willey and Phillips (1958:22):

> ...an archaeological unit possessing traits sufficiently characteristic to distinguish it from all other units similarly conceived, whether of the same or other cultures or civilizations, spatially limited to the order of magnitude of a locality or region and chronologically limited to a relatively brief interval of time.

In a seminal paper on the concept of phase, Donald Abbott (1972) vigorously points out the flaws with the above definition and the use of phase on the Northwest Coast. Firstly, Abbott notes Willey and Phillips', albeit reserved, linkage between phase and society. According to Willey and Phillips (1958:49) "[T]he equivalent of phase, then, ought to be 'society'". Abbott does not equate phase and society for two major reasons.

First, seasonal movements to different resource extraction areas by a cultural group would be reflected in the archaeological record as distinct, seasonally specific assemblages (Abbott 1972, Suttles 1951). In reality the different archaeological assemblages would represent one cultural group at differing times of the year. Therefore, one society may have more than one phase attributed to it during the same time period, thus contradicting the definition of Willey and Phillips.

Abbott (1972) felt that the Locarno Beach and Marpole units could actually be seasonal variants of the same cultural group. At the time of his article ambiguity in chronometric dating made his beliefs possible. However, the distribution of radiocarbon dates has since shown a temporal separation of the two archaeological units with Locarno Beach predating Marpole (Burley 1980).

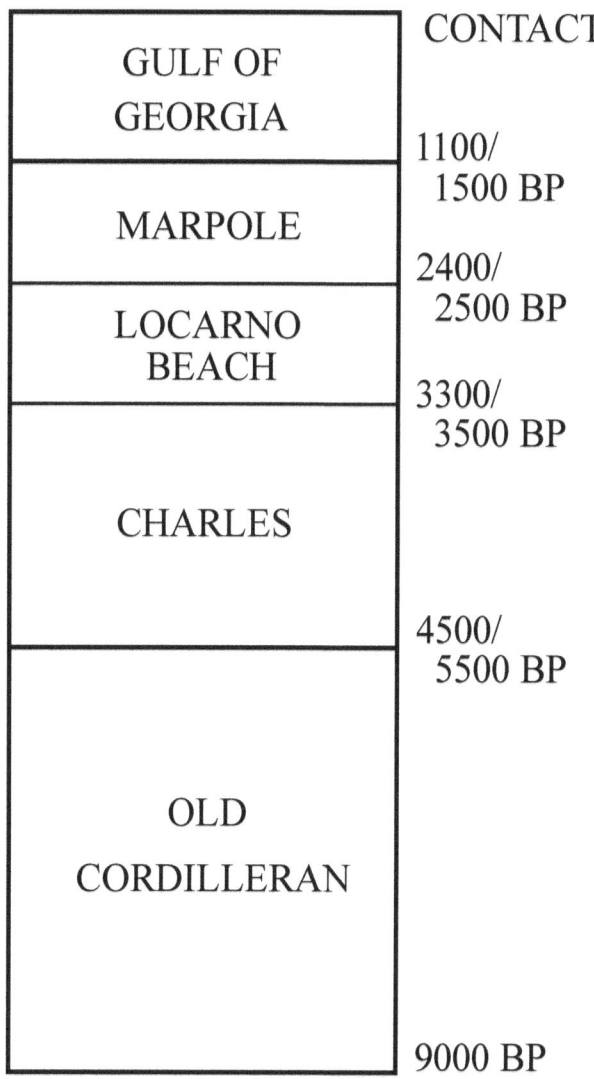

Figure 2.1 Gulf of Georgia Regional Culture History

Abbott's (1972) second issue with phase is that similarity of assemblages may reflect economic practicality rather than ethnic affiliation. Dale Croes (1987, 1992, Croes and Hackenberger 1988) furthers the point by claiming that Locarno Beach and Marpole are economic plateaus and have no distinct and different cultural affiliation. If similar assemblages are grouped together as a phase, then correlation between a phase and a single discrete society must be challenged.

Although Abbott's (1972) first assumption about the seasonal relationship turned out to be incorrect, both of his problems with the use of phase are important in Northwest Coast archaeology. Seasonally-specific archaeological assemblages could serve to split prehistoric cultures into more than one phase and economic practicality could lump more than one cultural group together. These two factors skewing archaeological phases in distinctly different directions would then seriously question the utility of the concept of phase on the Northwest Coast.

While most Northwest Coast archaeologists accept Abbott's reservations about the concept of phase, the term remains in widespread usage (Burley 1980). Although the direct link between phase and society is spurious, phase as an archaeological unit still has classificatory value. In *Clustering and Scaling of Gulf of Georgia Sites*, Matson (1974) examined the nature of variation in the Gulf of Georgia regional sequence. He found that although the phase relationships were built on an *ad hoc* subjective basis they did have statistical strength. Matson's study (1974) upheld the discrimination of three separate archaeological units. Locarno Beach, Marpole and the subsequent Gulf of Georgia grouped independently of each other in terms of assemblage variability (Matson 1974). Further, radiocarbon dates have shown a temporal differentiation that strengthens the formal argument (Burley 1980). Thus, although archaeologists do not clearly understand what phase would mean in emic terms there seems to be valid grounds in using the concept as a means of classification.

In a paper titled *Method and Theory in Northwest Coast Archaeology*, Roy Carlson (1983) states that he and Charles Borden chose to employ the term phase but never accepted the societal baggage that Willey and Phillips (1958) added to it. For Carlson phase does not imply society. He used phase as "a working tool ... that ... is defined on the basis of culture content, not on time and space." (1983:33).

To avoid the phase problem altogether Donald Mitchell offered culture type to describe the segments of the regional sequence. Influenced by Albert Spaulding, Mitchell's "culture type is a conveniently vague term... which means a component is distinguished by common possession of a group of traits" (Spaulding 1955:12). Similar to the Willey and Phillips definition of phase, culture type is defined on the similarity of shared traits. Both terms are subjective as each archaeologist may conceive the amount of variation between assemblages differently and may not group them together into the same phases. Mitchell's use of culture type however, does not imply a direct connection to a past social entity or a period of time. Although he developed the term to serve the direct culture historical approach, culture type does not necessarily mean prehistoric culture.

If we compare Carlson's (1983) version of Willey and Phillips' (1958) phase with that of Mitchell's (1971b) culture type we see little in the way of difference. Both terms are arbitrary boundaries placed around similar components in the archaeological record. Both phase and culture type, delineate formal patterns of association between assemblages independent of time and space. Both terms function as classificatory tools rather than descriptions of past societies.

The phase-culture type debate was described by Carlson (1983:33): "[a]nyone attempting to disentangle the taxonomic picture might well conclude that above the level of component Northwest Coast archaeologists don't know what they are talking about."

However, many archaeologists use different terms but mean the same thing. Even though Northwest Coast archaeologists use both phase and culture type as descriptive categories for archaeological assemblages there is little debate over the regional sequence to which they apply. The definition of Locarno Beach, for instance, whether defined as a phase or as a culture type is generally well established in the literature. The difference between phase and culture type is a semantic one which, in the field of Northwest Coast archaeology, is imperceptible.

My choice of which term I will use in this thesis is also arbitrary. I will follow Mitchell (1971b) and use culture type for two reasons. First, I feel Abbott (1972) makes a stronger argument not to use phase than do Willey and Phillips (1958) for not using culture type. Abbott (1972) argues correctly, that the link between phase and prehistoric society is spurious, yet the definition of phase has strong connotations of prehistoric society. Willey and Phillips (1958) feel culture type should be reserved as a more generalizing term to be used to describe classes of phases.

Second, Mitchell's (1971b) use of Spaulding's (1955) culture type comes without modification. The use of phase is consistently cited as the Willey and Phillips (1958) definition although apparently Carlson (1983) and

Borden employed a modified version. There is ambiguity in the use of phase as two definitions coexist in the region. Although most archaeologists cite Willey and Phillips (1958), I feel that the way phase is used more closely follows Carlson's (1983) version of the term.

As mentioned previously the meaning of phase or culture type is debated. The direct link to past society has been challenged and rejected (Abbott 1972, Croes 1987, 1992). If phases or cultures types do not represent prehistoric societies then what do they represent? For this thesis I will follow the meaning argued for by Croes (1987, Croes and Hackenberger 1988), that is, economic practicality. Culture types reflect a suite of technological adaptations to best exploit a particular subsistence pattern in a given environment. Thus they may be independent of ethnicity.

Evidence supporting this position comes from basketry and artifact remains at a series of sites near Hoko River, Washington. Croes (1987) discovered that basketry style and culture type do not co-vary. Basket weaving has long been seen as an indicator of ethnicity as basketry style does not affect function (Croes 1987). Thus weaving style can be seen as an ethnic marker. The artifact assemblage of the Hoko River sites was consistent with the Locarno Beach culture type of the Gulf of Georgia, but the basketry styles had clear affinities with sites on the West Coast of Vancouver Island where the artifact assemblages are very different. Croes (1987) argues that the Hoko River sites represent people associated culturally to the West Coast of Vancouver Island, probably Wakashan speakers but employing a Locarno Beach toolkit. These people were probably ethnically and linguistically distinct from the other Gulf of Georgia populations which also used the Locarno Beach culture type assemblage.

A visual representation of this notion can be seen in Figure 2.2, (see also Chapter Three). This diagram shows the successive plateaus which correspond to the culture type of the regional sequence. Croes and Hackenberger (1988) argue population increased gradually in the region until the carrying capacity of a particular economy was surpassed. Technological adaptation allowed for a rapid increase in population which marked the development of a new culture type.

Thus culture types are not necessarily culturally determined and emically important distinctions. They are however invaluable classificatory tools. They allow archaeologists the ability to conceive of a long unpredictable set of culture historical events in manageable segments. Beyond that, the culture types also have statistical strength. As mentioned, Matson (1974) found that Locarno Beach, Marpole and Gulf of Georgia culture types are statistically valid units of analysis.

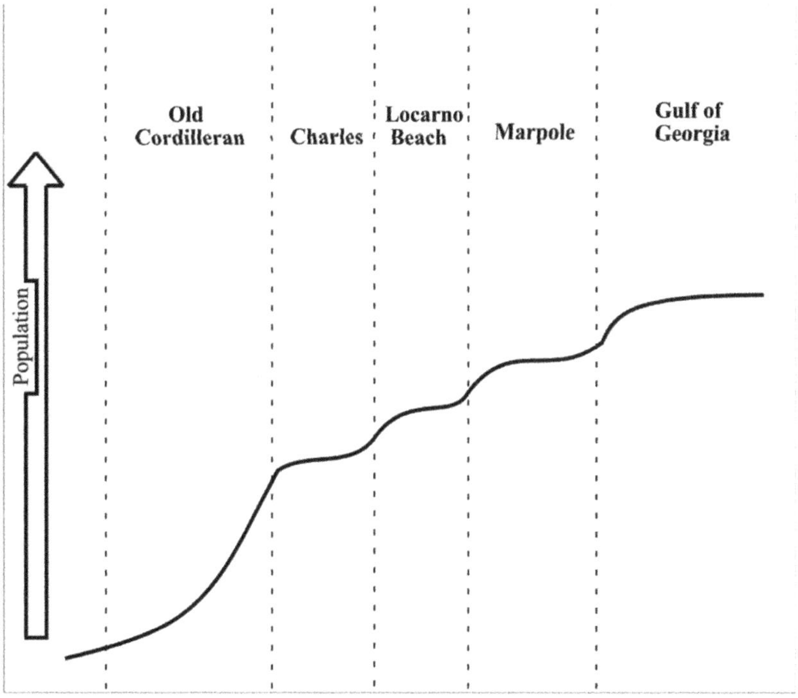

My definitions of Locarno Beach culture type, Marpole culture type and the subphases of Marpole are listed later in this chapter. As there is little debate regarding these groupings and most Northwest Coast archaeologists use the definitions that I cite, I feel confident in using them. The phase/ culture type question deals with the meaning of said groupings and since I acknowledge Abbott's criticism (1972) of the link between phase and society I choose culture type as my unit of analysis. I envision culture type as per Croes (1987, Croes and Hackenberger 1988), an economic and technological plateau adaptation to a given situation.

The field of Northwest Coast Archaeology is due for some theoretical introspection wherein questions of phase and culture type should be explicitly addressed and a reworked and less *ad hoc* typology should be developed. As it stands, the field functions adequately

Figure 2.2 Croes and Hackenberger's Economic Plateaus Model of Gulf of Georgia Population and Culture Change. after Croes and Hackenberger 1988:75.

with archaeologists able to communicate their results effectively. With this in mind, it seems unlikely that anyone would attempt to create a more uniform typology and powerful theoretical baseline, thus I will draw from the existing knowledge base for this thesis, while acknowledging it to be somewhat flawed.

Culture Types

Mitchell (1971b) formulated the Locarno Beach and Marpole culture types with an eye towards a Gulf of Georgia regional sequence. He based his definitions on the excavated components for both the Locarno Beach and Marpole culture types at the time of his publication. The data upon which the definition of the Marpole culture type is based is not representative of the entire Gulf of Georgia, but is skewed toward Fraser River sites. The majority of excavated sites are located near the mouth of the Fraser River. Thus Marpole is a Fraser River-centric construct, and Marpole is difficult to recognize in peripheral areas.

The Locarno Beach culture type also suffers from an unrepresentative definition as it is weighted toward Gulf Island sites and thus instead of a Fraser River bias it may be Gulf Islands-centric (Matson and Coupland 1995).

These issues of representativeness may be an artifact of uneven archaeological research or they may be related to actual changing cultural use patterns in the Gulf of Georgia region. In either case, the accepted definitions of Locarno Beach and Marpole culture types may not be applicable across the entire Gulf. Variations within each culture type, both spatially and temporally, exist and the current definitions often minimize that fact.

In an attempt to grapple with variation within Marpole assemblages, Matson et al. (1980) developed three subphases of Marpole. Assemblage variability is explained in temporal and geographic terms. This thesis will continue this process by reworking the Matson et al. (1980) study with the addition of Southern Vancouver Island sites to examine wider geographic variation for the Locarno Beach and Marpole culture types.

The next section serves to outline the state of current knowledge of the Locarno Beach and Marpole culture types. Information regarding the technological adaptation, subsistence strategy, settlement structure and geographic and temporal extent of both Locarno Beach and Marpole culture types will be discussed. The definitions of Locarno Beach and Marpole presented in this chapter will be referred to throughout the remainder of the thesis.

The Locarno Beach Culture Type
Technology

Charles Borden (1950, 1951) first proposed the Locarno Beach phase as part of his Early Period based on his work at the Locarno Beach site and Whalen Farm. Three things were clear to Borden: Locarno Beach was old, it was "Eskimoid" in nature, and it was focused on sea mammal hunting. (Borden 1950, 1951, Drucker 1955, 1958). Borden saw an "Eskimoid" character to the artifact assemblages from Locarno Beach I and Whalen I and felt Locarno Beach represented an "Eskimo-aleut" migration or diffused influence into the area (Matson 1989).

Borden's Intermediate Period, which will be discussed later in this chapter, consisted of the Marpole-Point Grey-Locarno Beach I and Whalen II site components (Borden 1950, 1951). This period was seen as the product of another migration, this time from the Interior.

Under heavy criticism (Osbourne, Caldwell and Crabtree 1956) and swayed by new evidence, the "Eskimoid" origin of Locarno Beach and the Interior origin of Marpole were abandoned in Borden's 1962 *West Coast Crossties with Alaska*. It was six years later that Borden drew together a clear picture of the Locarno Beach phase (Borden 1968a). His Early Period became the Locarno Beach phase.

Based on data from Borden (1950, 1951, 1960, 1962, 1968b, and particularly 1970) and from excavations at Montague Harbour (Mitchell 1971b), Helen Point (Carlson 1970) and Bowker Creek (Mitchell 1979), Mitchell (1971b) presented the diagnostic features of the Locarno Beach culture type. This list of 19 traits (see Table 2.1) has been adopted in many other subsequent studies (e.g. McMurdo 1974, Charlton 1980, Capes 1977, Percy 1974, Trace 1981) The concept of Locarno Beach phase as developed by Borden (1950, 1951 and 1970) and refined by Mitchell (1971b) into the Locarno Beach culture type is widely utilized within the Gulf of Georgia region. In this study the defining characteristics of Locarno Beach culture type as defined by Mitchell (1971b:57) will be followed throughout this thesis.

Table 2.1 Locarno Beach Diagnostic Traits
(1) Medium-sized chipped-basalt points, many with contracting stems.
(2) Microblades and cores.
(3) Chipped slate or sandstone knives or scrapers of generally ovoid or ulu shape.
(4) Crude cobble, split cobble, and boulder spall implements.
(5) Large, faceted ground-slate points and similar points of bone.
(6) Thick ground-slate knives, often only partially ground.

(7) Small, well-made celts rectangular in plan and cross-section.
(8) Gulf Islands complex artifacts of as yet unknown function—produced in a variety of forms, some of which seem to fall within definable, if broad types (Duff 1956).
(9) Labrets of several forms.
(10) Earspools.
(11) Grooved or notched sinkers.
(12) Handstones and grinding slabs.
(13) Heavy bone wedges.
(14) Bilaterally barbed antler points.
(15) Toggling harpoons of unarmed, one-piece toggling or composite form.
(16) Antler foreshafts for the above harpoons.
(17) Sea mussel shell celts.
(18) Clay-lined depressions and alignments of vertically placed rock slabs.
(19) Sometimes associated with a now "inland" location and with deposits containing little shell or shell which is much decomposed.

Subsistence

The Locarno Beach culture type artifact assemblage paints the picture of a full maritime adaptation (Burley 1980, Trace 1981). The hunting of sea mammals and fishing is evident from the artifactual assemblage. Composite toggling harpoon valves and foreshafts are implicated in the hunting of sea lions, porpoises and seals (Borden 1950, 1951, 1970, Borden and Archer 1974). Further, Dale Croes (1976) interpreted long lengths of cordage recovered at the Musqueam Northeast site as retrieving lines for sea mammal hunting harpoons.

Charles Borden (1951) felt Locarno Beach represented a primarily sea mammal hunting society with land mammal, birds, fish and shellfish as important secondary food resources. More recent and scientific faunal analyses (Steifel 1985, Wigen 1980) found that land and sea mammals do provide the most significant portions of known subsistence. Shellfish, salmon, herring and other fish were also important in Locarno Beach subsistence. The technology to preserve and store salmon developed in the Locarno Beach culture type (Matson 1992, Pratt 1992). The diagnosis of salmon storage can be accomplished by the systematic recovery and analysis of salmon bones. Where the ratio of cranial to post-cranial bones is very small, salmon storage can be inferred (Boehm 1973, Wigen 1980, Butler 1983). This is based on the ethnographic pattern of the removal of the salmon head prior to drying (Suttles 1955). Thus the point of consumption of stored salmon should show an abnormally low ratio of cranial to post-cranial skeletal elements.

Herring was also noted as a meaningful portion of subsistence at numerous sites (Steifel 1985, Wigen 1980, Mitchell 1979, Mitchell 1988b, Matson 1992, and Stewart n.d.).

It should be noted here and in every reference to prehistoric subsistence on the Northwest Coast that evidence for plant use in the archaeological record is at best, sketchy. The contribution of plant material to the diet during Locarno Beach times is not well known. Poor preservation, recovery problems and lack of study have all served to devalue the importance of flora in the Northwest Coast archaeological record. All that can be validly stated is that it is certainly underrepresented in reconstructions of subsistence.

Settlement

Whereas there is substantial evidence for the location and seasonality of sites, very little archaeological evidence exists to illuminate the nature of Locarno Beach settlement, known sites of which are plotted on Figure 2.3. These sites are generally not associated with the mouth of the Fraser River, rather they are almost exclusively oriented towards offshore resources (Mitchell 1971b). R.G. Matson (1992, et al. 1991) has documented a pit house at Crescent Beach. One other possible pit house has been reported at Sequim, Washington (Morgan 1998, 1999). In addition, several post mould features have been noted at Long Harbour (Johnstone 1991) and Shoemaker Bay (McMillan and St. Claire 1982). These bits of fragmentary evidence are all that can describe Locarno Beach habitation. Little is known in the way of village structure or inter- and intra- household composition.

Status differences occur during Locarno Beach times and can be witnessed in differential burial inclusions and labret use. The use of labrets as personal adornment has been interpreted as a marker of high status (Cybulski 1991). As the use of these lip ornaments can be initiated in adulthood, the nature of status differential is not understood. In later time periods status markers, such as cranial deformation are clearly associated with ascribed and not achieved status. Burley and Knusel (1989) conclude that there is no clear evidence for ascribed status during the Locarno Beach culture type. However, according to Roy Carlson's (1987) burial analysis, grave inclusions are associated with subadult individuals, suggesting that ascribed status does occur within the Locarno Beach culture type. It is apparent that some status differentiation does occur during Locarno Beach and it is possible that ascribed status, although not widespread, is developing.

Sites

The Locarno Beach culture type is represented across the Gulf of Georgia region by at least 28 sites. Table 2.2,

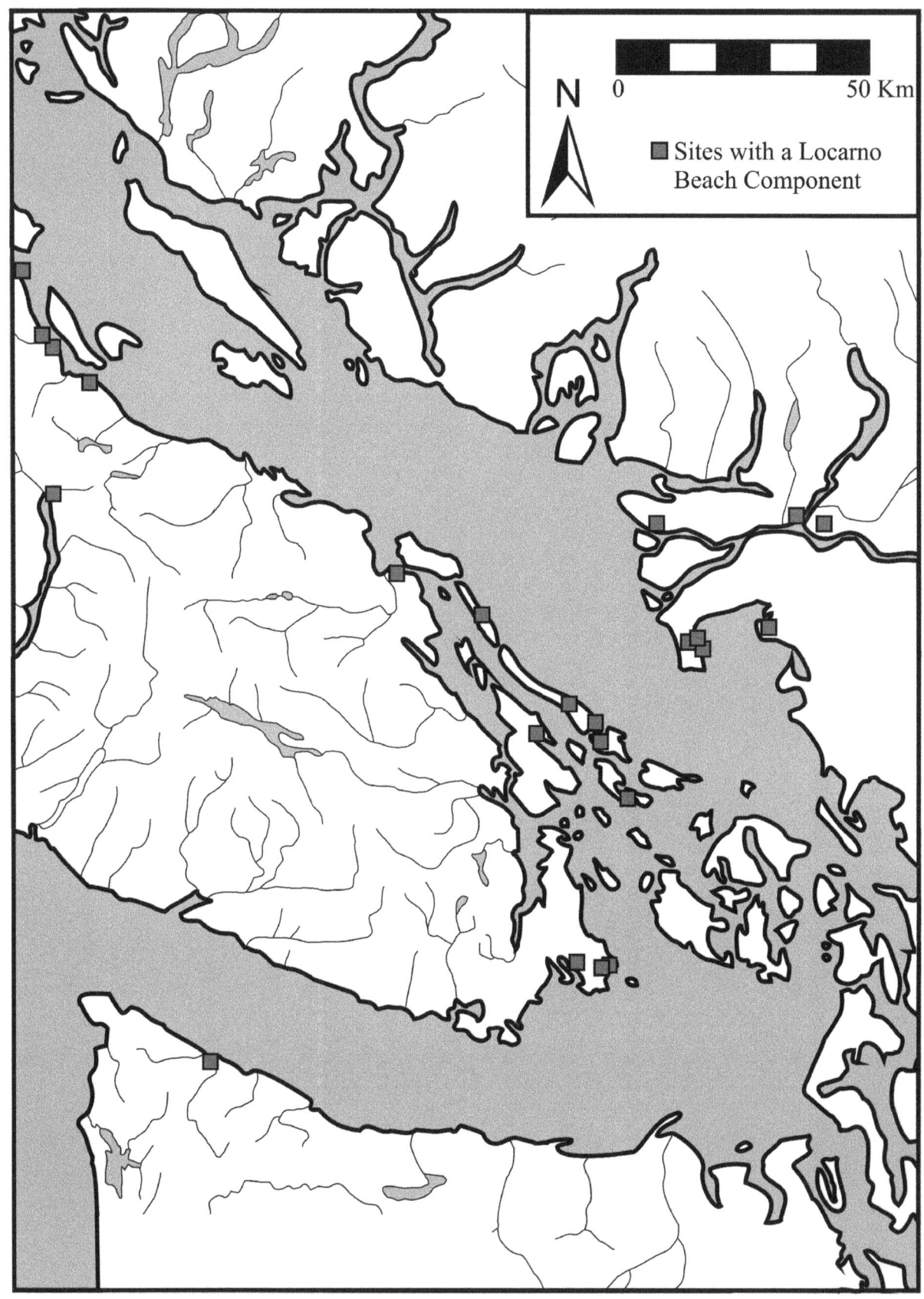

Figure 2.3 Map of Locarno Beach Culture Type Components

Table 2.2 Archaeological Sites with a Known Locarno Beach Component

Site	Reference	Site	Reference
Willows Beach	Kenny 1974	Telep	Peacock 1982
Belcarra Park	Charlton 1980	Buckley Bay	Mitchell 1974
Jack Point	Murray 1982	Tsable River Bridge	Wigen 1980
J. Puddleduck	Mitchell 1988b	Marpole	Burley 1979, Pratt 1992
Montague Harbour I	Mitchell 1971b	Beach Grove North	Ball 1979
Little Beach	Arcas 1991a	Deep Bay	Monks 1977
Shoemaker Bay I	McMillan and St. Claire 1982	Millard Creek	Capes 1977
Hoko River	Croes 1989	Tsawwassen	Arcas 1991b
Pender Canal	Carlson 1986, Hanson 1990	Locarno Beach	Borden 1950, 1951, Pratt 1991
Long Harbour	Johnstone 1991	Whalen Farm	Borden 1950, 1951, Thom and Matson 1991
Bowker Creek	Mitchell 1979	Musqueam NE	Borden 1976, Borden and Archer 1974
Georgeson Bay	Haggarty and Sendey 1976	Crescent Beach	Percy 1974, Trace 1981, Matson et al. 1991
Helen Point	McMurdo 1976	Simonarson	Gaston 1975
Valdes Island	Apland 1981	Kosapsom	Mitchell 1995, 1996
Pitt River	Patenaude 1985	Sequim	Morgan 1996, 1998, 1999

after Matson and Coupland 1995:157

shows the Locarno Beach assemblages identified at present. The sites cover the range of the Gulf of Georgia region with many of the sites in the Gulf Islands. Figure 2.3, shows the placement of archaeological sites with Locarno Beach components across the Gulf of Georgia.

Dating
Several dozen radiocarbon dates are available for Locarno Beach and the temporal extent appears to be from 3500/3300 BP to 2400 BP (Matson and Coupland 1995, Mitchell 1990, Burley 1980). Refer to Figure 2.1, for a graphic representation of the position of Locarno Beach within the Gulf of Georgia regional culture historical sequence.

The Marpole Culture Type
Technology
The development of the Marpole culture type as a theoretical construct follows the development of Locarno Beach culture type. The Intermediate Period arose from the early work of Charles Borden (1950, 1951), and was later changed into the Marpole phase (Borden 1970). Originally thought to be an intrusive Interior adaptation, it later was seen as an *in situ* development from Locarno Beach phase. The Marpole culture type was first presented in Mitchell (1971b). Here again, Mitchell (1971b) followed Borden (1950a, 1951, 1960, 1962, 1968b, and particularly 1970) and drew together a coherent attribute list for Marpole. Mitchell's (1971b:52) diagnostic trait list follows:

Table 2.3 Marpole Diagnostic Traits
(1) Chipped-stone points in a number of forms, both stemmed and unstemmed; most of "medium" size, but some large-leaf shapes occur; a common small basalt variety is asymmetrically triangular.
(2) Microblades.
(3) Large ground-slate points, some faceted, others of lenticular cross-section.
(4) Thin ground-slate fish knives, plentiful at Fraser River sites but much less common at sites outside this area.
(5) Celts of various sizes, generally large, made with little care, of flattened oval cross-section and with a rough, rounded poll; the sides often taper toward the poll.
(6) Disk beads of clamshell or shale.
(7) Labrets and, possibly, earspools (inferred from sculpture).
(8) Stone hand mauls, well made and with nipple or other decoration on top.
(9) Perforated stones, both large and small; handstones.
(10) Stone sculpture, including decorated bowls, large heads with depressions in the top; seated human figures, decorated pipe bowls, incised siltstone, and fish effigies.
(11) Large needles.
(12) Sectioned or split bone awls.
(13) Barbed, non-toggling harpoon points with a tang for attachment to shaft and line guards and (or) line hole; most are unilaterally barbed.
(14) Unilaterally barbed antler points, equivalent to the unilaterally barbed bone points of the Gulf of Georgia culture but in general somewhat larger and with larger barbs.
(15) Antler wedges.

(16) Antler sculpture.
(17) Relatively frequent use of native copper for ornaments.
(18) Midden burial, with positions ranging from loosely to tightly flexed; some burials with plentiful inclusions; dentalia, disk beads, native copper, large points, etc.; some with cairns.
(19) Skull deformation and occasional trepanation.
(20) Large post moulds and house outlines.

David Burley's (1979) doctoral dissertation (Burley 1980) was the first monograph-length publication to look directly at a single culture type on the Northwest Coast (Matson and Coupland 1995). Using a multidimensional scalar analysis and a trait list of 51 diagnostic features (see Table 5.3), Burley examined the nature of Marpole technology. Major differences in Marpole culture type traits from those of Locarno Beach are the proliferation of art and wealth objects, changes in harpoon styles, raw materials, and the presence of large house structures within larger sites.

The Burley (1980) typology was later used in Matson et al.'s (1980) subsequent study on Marpole variability. This thesis adds to both of these previous studies and as such I will employ Burley's (1980) typology for the sake of uniformity.

Subsistence

Data on the subsistence of the Marpole culture type is limited. Three sites that have been well reported are Glenrose Cannery (Matson 1976, 1981), Crescent Beach (Matson et al. 1991, Matson 1992) and Deep Bay (Monks 1977, 1987). From these sites a tentative reconstruction of subsistence is possible. Stored salmon provided a large portion of the diet which was focused towards marine resources. Flatfish and clams provided seasonal supplements when available (Matson et al. 1991, Matson 1992). Herring was extensively harvested where runs were abundant (Monks 1977, 1987). As during Locarno Beach, the contribution of plant resources to diet is poorly understood.

Settlement

Compared to the preceding culture type relatively more is known about Marpole settlement. The platforms associated with large plank houses are visible at Garrison (Kornbacher 1989), Beach Grove (Matson et al. 1980), False Narrows (Burley 1989), Whalen Farm (Smith 1921), Dionisio Point (Mitchell 1971a), and possibly Tualdad Altu (Chatters 1989). Further, large post moulds have been found at Marpole (Borden 1970) and

Table 2.4 Archaeological Sites with a Known Marpole Component

Site	Reference	Site	Reference
Montague Harbour II	Mitchell 1971b	Whalen Farm	Seymour 1976, Thom 1992
Helen Point II	J. McMurdo 1974	Birch Bay	Gaston 1975
Cadboro Bay I	Mitchell 1968a	Cherry Point	Gaston 1975
False Narrows	Burley 1989	Nooksack	Grabert and Larsen 1975
Marpole	Burley 1979, Smith 1903, Borden 1970	Bellingham Bay	Burley 1980
Old Musqueam	Monks 1976	Hill Site	Hall and Haggarty 1981
Beach Grove	Borden 1970, Matson et al. 1980	Birds Eye Cove	Wilmeth 1978, Burley 1980
Point Grey	Matson 1974, Coupland 1991	Dionisio Point	Mitchell 1971a
Garrison	Carlson 1960, Kornbacher 1989	Argyle Lagoon	Carlson 1960
Richardson	Carlson 1960	Maple Bank	A. McMurdo 1976
Cattle Point	Carlson 1960	Fox Cove	Kidd 1969
North Saanich	Smith 1907	Locarno Beach	Borden 1950
Deep Bay	Monks 1977, 1987	Tsawwassen	Arcas 1991b
Shoemaker Bay I	McMillan and St. Claire 1982	Water Hazard Site	Bernick 1989
Musqueam Northeast	Matson 1974	Long Harbour	Johnstone 1991
Glenrose Cannery	Matson 1976	Biederbost	Nordquist 1976
Port Hammond	Smith 1907	St. Mungo	Calvert 1970, Boehm 1973
Sumas	Grabert and Larsen 1975	Liquid Air	Sneed 1970
Crescent Beach	Percy 1974, Matson et al. 1991	Pender Canal	Hanson 1990, Carlson 1986, 1990b
English Bluff	Sutherland n.d.	Duke Point	Murray 1982

after Matson and Coupland 1995:202

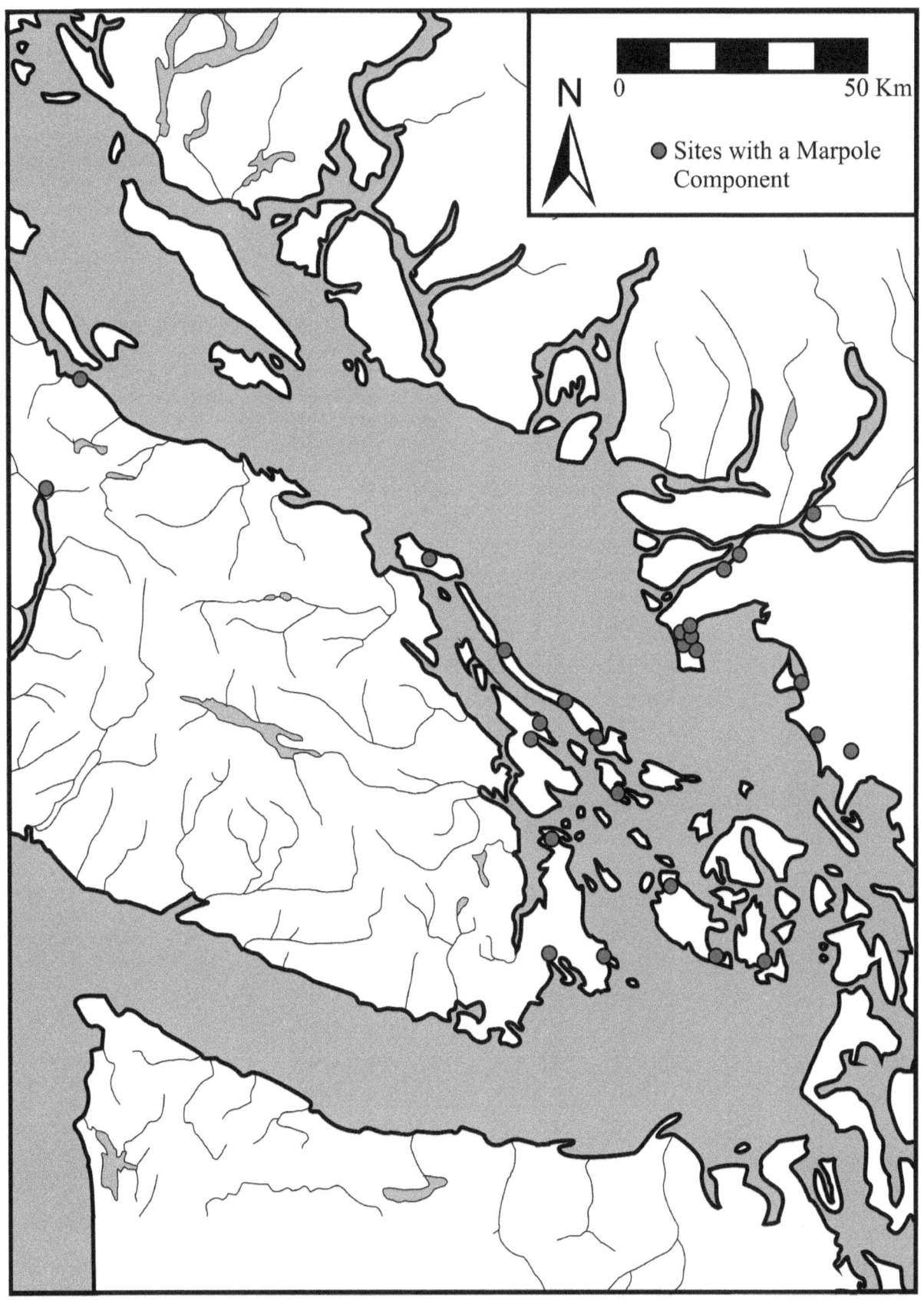

Figure 2.4 Map of Marpole Culture Type Components

Shoemaker Bay (McMillan and St. Claire 1982). These post moulds are massive enough to possibly be associated with large plank houses.

Seasonality studies have shown season-specific site use. Crescent Beach has been affiliated with winter and spring occupation and is dominated by stored salmon (Matson et al. 1991, Matson 1992). Glenrose Cannery has been interpreted as a spring flatfish and clam harvesting settlement (Matson 1976, 1981). Lastly, Deep Bay seems to be a focused area of herring exploitation during seasonal runs (Monks 1977, 1987).

Clear evidence of ascribed status can be inferred from the presence of cranial deformation during Marpole (Cybulski 1991, Burley and Knusel 1989). R.G. Matson (1976) and Burley and Knusel (1989) feel sub-adult burial inclusions also point to ascribed status in Marpole.

Sites
Matson and Coupland (1995) identify 40 Marpole sites in the Gulf of Georgia. The number of sites increases with Marpole and many of these sites occur near the Fraser River. Table 2.5, lists the sites believed to possess a Marpole culture type component and Figure 2.4 plots these sites within the Gulf of Georgia.

Dating
Several dozen radiocarbon dates have been analyzed for Marpole and the temporal extent appears to be from 2400 BP to 1500/1100 BP (Matson and Coupland 1995, Mitchell 1990, Burley 1980). There is some ambiguity as to the decline of Marpole and the incipience of Gulf of Georgia, shown in the 400 years transitionary period.

The Subphases of Marpole
Matson et al. (1980), using slightly modified data from Burley (1980), advanced a three subphase scheme to explain variability within the Marpole culture type. Employing similar multidimensional scalar techniques to those used by Matson (1974) and Burley (1980), Matson et al. (1980) named the Old Musqueam, Beach Grove and Garrison subphases of Marpole. The results of their analysis are shown in Table 2.5 and Figures 2.5, 2.6 and 2.7. The distribution of the three Marpole subphases is plotted in Figure 2.8.

Figure 2.5, shows the first two dimensions of multidimensional scaling. As can be seen, there are three distinct clusters which represent the three subphases of Marpole. Twenty well documented site components from across the Gulf of Georgia region which employed the Burley (1980) typology were used in this study. Figure 2.6, shows cluster analysis of the output of dimensions one and two of multidimensional scaling. This dendrogram shows a clearer picture of how the site

Table 2.5 Subphases of Marpole Site Components

Site Component	Borden or U.S. Site #	Abbreviation Used	Subphase
Montague Harbour II	DfRu 13	MH2	Garrison
False Narrows I	DgRw 4	FN1	Garrison
Garrison	45SJ25	G	Garrison
False Narrows II	DgRw 4	FN2	Garrison
Beach Grove 57,61,79	DgRs 1	BG 57,61,79	Garrison
Deep Bay II	DiSe 7	DB2	Garrison
English Bluff	DgRs 11	EB	Garrison
Point Grey	DhRt 5	PG	Garrison
Helen Point IIA	DfRu 8	HP2A	Beach Grove
Helen Point IIB	DfRu 8	HP2B	Beach Grove
Hill Site	DfRu 4	HS	Beach Grove
Whalen Farm	DfRs 1	WF	Beach Grove
Marpole II	DhRs 1	M2	Beach Grove
Beach Grove 80	DgRs 1	BG 80	Beach Grove
Beach Grove 62	DgRs 1	BG 62	Beach Grove
Crescent Beach III	DgRr 1	CB3	Old Musqueam
Fossil Bay I	45SJ105	FB1	Old Musqueam
Musqueam NE	DhRt 4	MNE	Old Musqueam
Old Musqueam	DhRt 1	OM	Old Musqueam
Glenrose Cannery III	DgRr 6	GC3	Old Musqueam

after: Matson et al. 1980:103

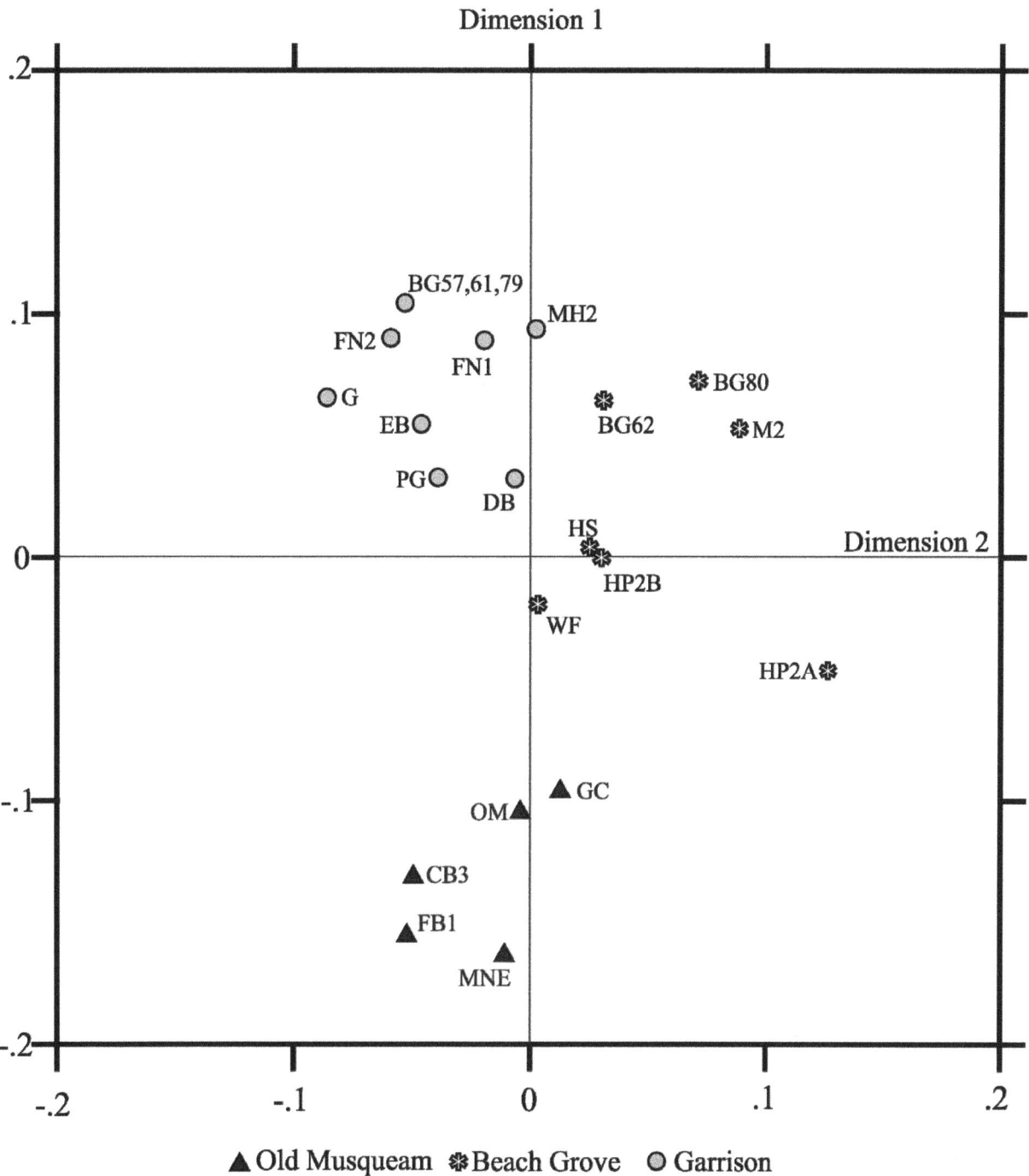

Figure 2.5 Dimensions 1 and 2 of Metric Multidimensional Scaling Results of 20 Marpole Components. After: Matson et al. 1980:103.

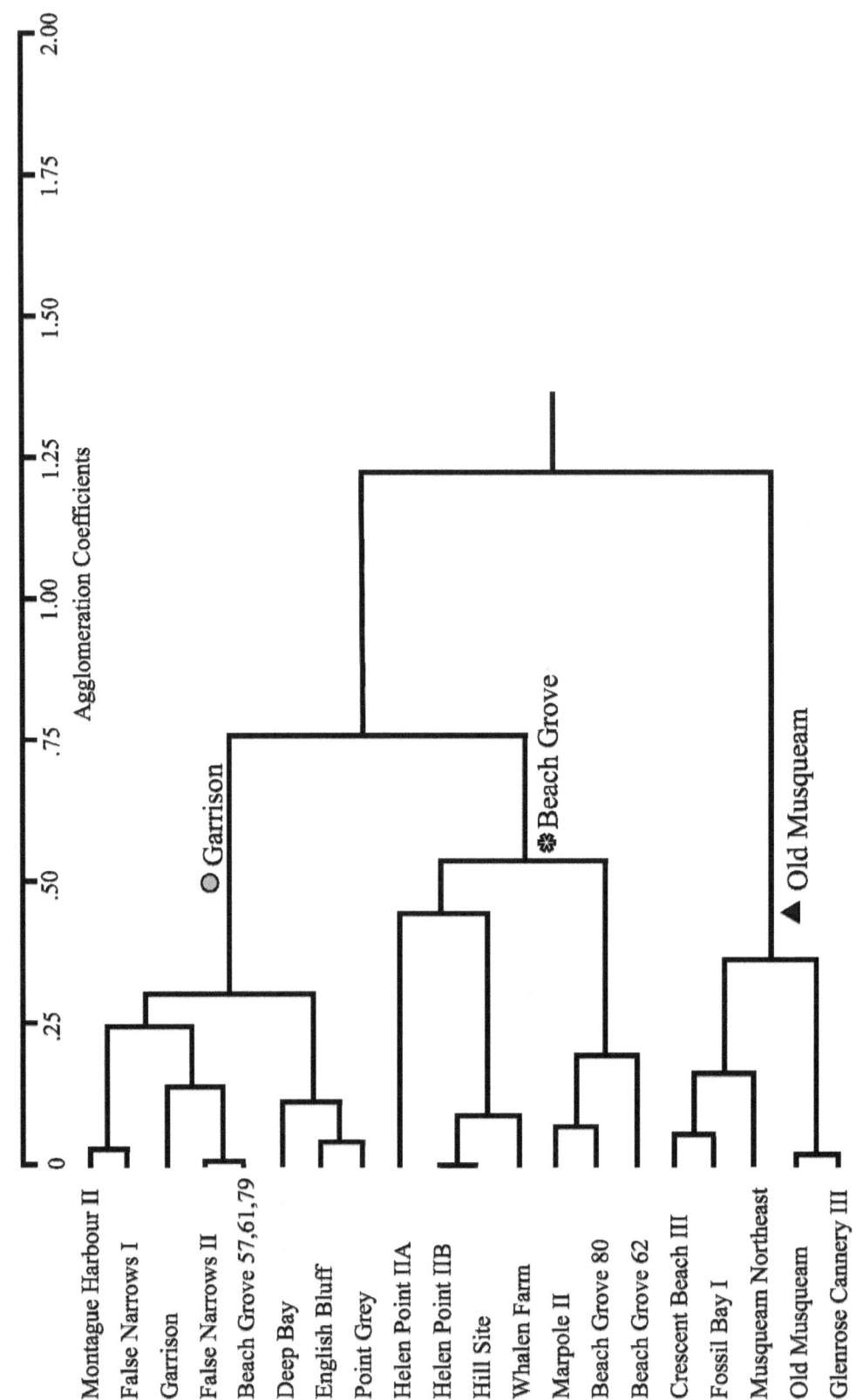

Figure 2.6 Ward's Cluster Analysis of Dimensions 1 and 2 of Metric Multidimensional Scaling Results of 20 Marpole Components.
After Matson et al. 1980:108

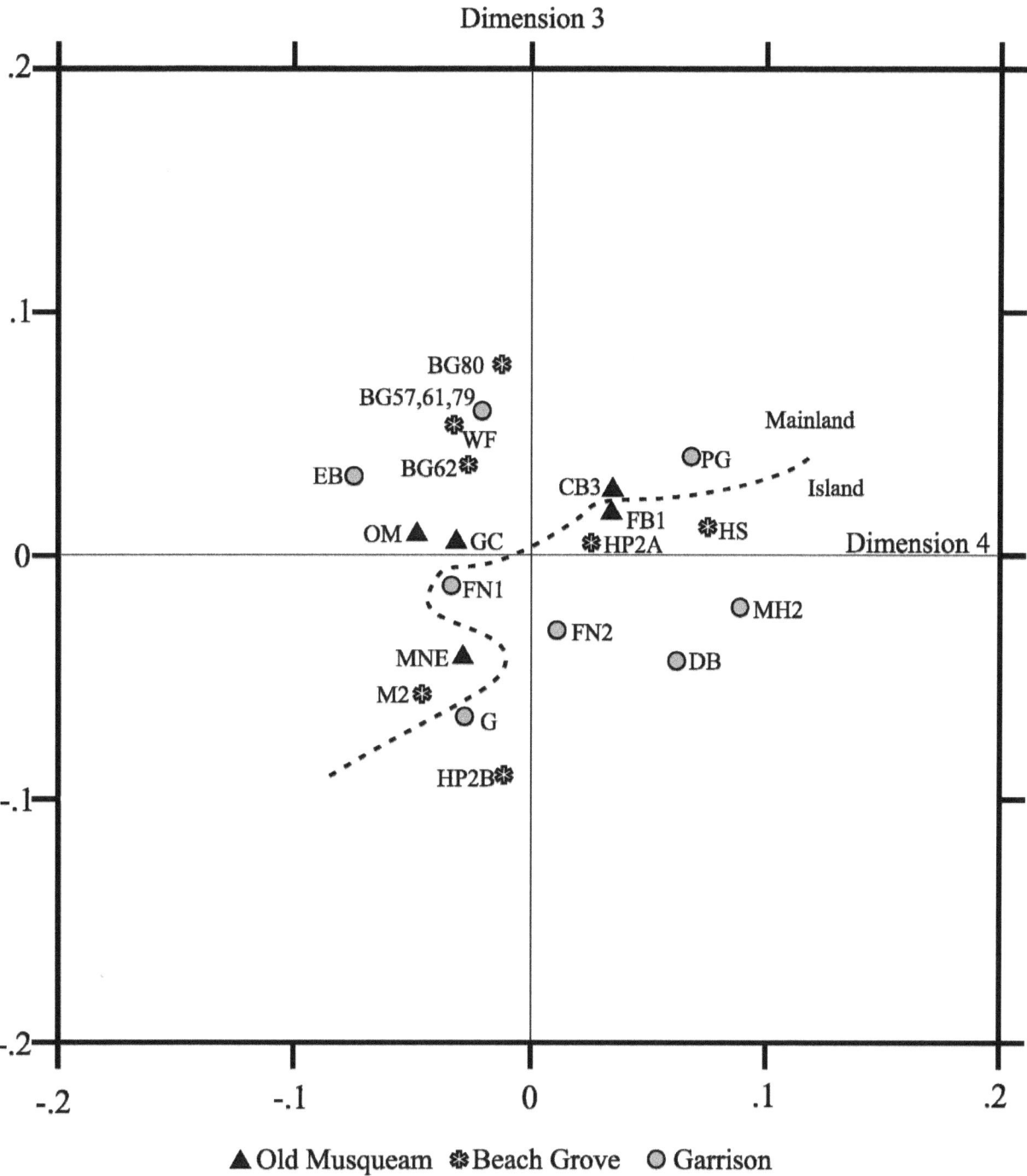

Figure 2.7 Dimensions 3 and 4 of Metric Multidimensional Scaling Results of 20 Marpole Components
After: Matson et al. 1980:106.

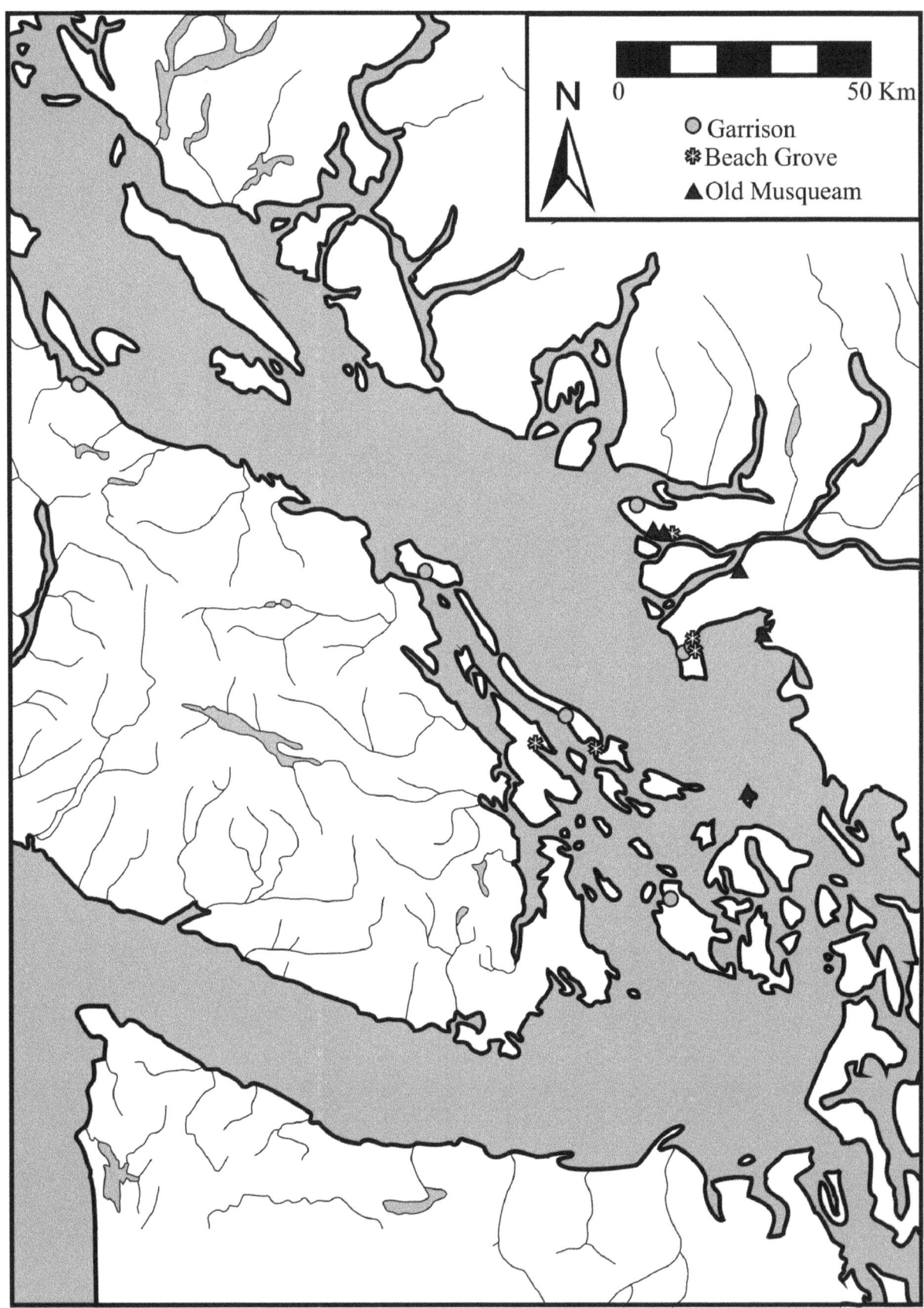

Figure 2.8 Map of Marpole Subphase Components

components are related. Figure 2.7, is the output of dimensions three and four of multidimensional scaling. Here a pattern that separates mainland from island sites is noted. This thesis adds new sites to the twenty site components used by Matson et al. (1980) and replicates the statistical procedures employed in that study (see Chapter Six). The Old Musqueam subphase has decidedly Locarno Beach-like attributes and the Garrison subphase is similar to the Gulf of Georgia culture type. Old Musqueam can be distinguished from Locarno Beach by having fewer cobble tools, shaped stone abraders, hammerstones, stone saws, bone chisels and wedges, and composite toggling harpoons (Matson et al. 1980, Matson and Coupland 1995). More traditionally Marpole diagnostic artifacts such as hand mauls and unilaterally barbed harpoons are limited to Beach Grove and Garrison subphases.

The Garrison subphase is identified by a shift to non-lithic industries such as bone, antler and wood. This subphase is also noted as not having labrets and microblades which are diagnostic of Locarno Beach and Early Marpole. The Beach Grove subphase is a transitional phase between the Old Musqueam and Garrison subphases. Within this subphase, hand mauls, unilaterally barbed harpoons, cranial deformation and rich grave inclusions all appear in the archaeological record. Matson and Coupland (1995) note that as of yet there is little radiocarbon help in separating Beach Grove and Garrison subphases but stratigraphy at False Narrows enables them to place Beach Grove between Old Musqueam and Garrison subphases.

The subphases of Marpole may be seen as transitional steps on a continuum between the Locarno Beach and Gulf of Georgia culture types. Assemblages vary through time but a general trend of increase in non-lithic and composite tools is noted (Matson and Coupland 1995). There remains some ambiguity in the definitions of each subphase; however, they will be used in regard to the proposed study. It is possible that this thesis will provide a better understanding of the Marpole transition and perhaps one or more of the subphases of Marpole will also be refined and better understood as a result. It is also possible that new Southern Vancouver Island specific subphases may be discovered.

The preceding chapter defined Locarno Beach and Marpole culture types as well as the subphases of Marpole. These definitions will be used in subsequent sections and be integral in a description of the results. The next chapter discusses the shift from Locarno Beach to Marpole and possible explanations of why the transition happened.

CHAPTER 3. EXPLANATIONS OF PREHISTORIC CULTURE CHANGE

This chapter outlines some of the existing explanations of the Locarno Beach -Marpole transition. The explanations presented do not cover the entire spectrum of available explanations but do provide useful information in evaluating the distinctiveness of the archaeological record of Southern Vancouver Island.

As mentioned in the previous chapter, Marpole sees a marked increase in sociocultural complexity. The Locarno Beach - Marpole transition is a critical time period in the development of the hallmarks of historically and ethnographically documented Northwest Coast cultures. Marpole sees the apparent rise and/or intensification of resource specialization, sedentism, cooperative housing, hereditary ascribed status and wealth accumulation, all characteristic of contact period Northwest Coast cultures (Matson and Coupland 1995). In addition, a social system of ranking develops into what many call a chiefdom (Coupland 1985, Croes and Hackenberger 1988, Ames 1983). Incipient social classes are being created and entrenched in the social fabric (Donald 1985, Matson 1989).

The explanations of the Marpole transition presented in this chapter seek to explain not only a change in the culture historical sequence but also the processes by which sociocultural complexity develops. In several instances, the explanation presented is meant to describe the more general process of the rise of status inequality. These explanations however see status inequality as developing in consort with the Marpole transition and therefore implicitly explain the transition.

The explanations are grouped into two basic themes: (1) dislocation explanations (2) continuity explanations. For each theme several explanations from different archaeologists will be presented. These explanations are not discrete entities unto themselves. Each one builds on data and ideas of previous archaeologists, and there is much overlap in theoretical framework between the explanations. Differences emerge as archaeologists search for the root cause of the Marpole transition and which factors are merely concomitant.

Dislocation Explanations

The first general series of explanations of prehistoric culture change for the Gulf of Georgia deal with dislocation. Migration as an interpretation of culture change in the Gulf of Georgia is as old as the archaeological research itself (Hill-Tout 1895, 1903, 1904, 1905, 1907, Smith 1907). These dislocation explanations attempt to explain the Marpole transition in terms of population movement. The focus of interpretation is rapid change in the artifact assemblage at the Locarno Beach - Marpole interface. This change is seen as the product of a new people bringing new technology. Similarities with previous occupations are said to be the result of diffusion during population replacement.

These explanations take the general form of a coastally-adapted population often described as Eskimoid in character being replaced by an interior or Plateau population moving downstream from the Fraser River Canyon. Several researchers over the last one hundred years have come up with similar explanations focusing on this replacement.

Charles Hill-Tout (1895:112), believed in an "invasion of hostile people" based on his excavation at the Marpole site. He deduced that a population of "Eskimoid" people was replaced by an intrusive group. Hill-Tout (1895) based his findings on an analysis of head shape in burials, where he noted two distinct populations. The first group whom he associated with the Eskimoid toolkit was dolichocephalic, or long-headed. The intrusive group was seemingly brachycephalic, or broad-headed (Hill-Tout 1895, 1948). Hill-Tout provided very little information regarding where his burial specimens were recovered and only included measurements for two crania (Beattie 1985, Carlson 1990a). Although subjective and speculative, Hill-Tout's (1895, 1903, 1904, 1905, 1907 and 1948) work planted the dislocation seed in the minds of subsequent archaeologists.

Harlan Smith (1907, 1921 and 1929) was the archaeologist for the Jesup North Pacific Expedition headed by Franz Boas. In this capacity, Smith played a major role in excavating and documenting archaeological sites on the Northwest Coast. His excavations at Port Hammond and at the Marpole site led Smith to envision a migration into coastal areas by Interior peoples (Smith 1907). These people, he thought, brought with them a tool industry adapted to the Fraser River Canyon. He also found evidence for a population separation between round-headed people and long-headed people which followed Hill-Tout's classification (Smith 1907). Smith was less theoretically inclined than Hill-Tout, spending much more of his time on site description than on explanation of change. However, the common theme of an interior to coast migration was still evident.

Based on a misinterpretation of Boas (in Smith 1903), Philip Drucker (1943) saw the same head shape pattern as Hill-Tout (1895) (Carlson 1990). Drucker (1955) blended this revival of Hill-Tout's population replacement with archaeological data and surmised an older and more widespread coastal adapted "ice hunting stratum" was replaced by a Plateau or interior culture.

The first scientific excavations in the province were undertaken by Charles Borden in the 1940s and 1950s. Borden (1950, 1951, 1958, 1960) followed a similar theme as the other archaeologists previously mentioned. He also believed in a primary "Eskimoid" culture being replaced by an "Interior adapted" culture. Borden based his conclusions on excavations at a number of Gulf of Georgia sites (1950, 1951, 1958, 1960) and his excavation techniques were much more advanced and systematic than those of his predecessors. Although his excavations were precise his analysis, however, was still subjective and lacked modern scientific rigor.

Borden was seen by most as the "Father of British Columbian Archaeology" (Matson and Coupland 1995:vi) and his views held sway with little opposition until one of his students, Donald Mitchell (1971b), offered a well-argued continuity explanation. Borden himself softened his viewpoint of dislocation in later publications (1962, 1968a). After Mitchell's (1971b) refutation of Borden's Eskimoid-Interior migration explanation, discontinuity in the Gulf of Georgia was left for dead by virtually all Northwest Coast archaeologists (Burley 1980).

David Burley revisited the migration topic in his doctoral dissertation (1979, published as 1980). His explanation followed the basic themes of the previous discontinuity theorists but for the first time he argued population replacement with well documented and scientific data. Where earlier attempts at discussing head shape had been at best subjective, Burley now employed modern multivariate techniques from physical anthropology in his examination of crania. The result, according to Burley and Beattie (1987), is the separation of two prehistoric populations, one they termed Locarno and the second they called Salish. The Locarno population existed during Locarno Beach times and the Salish during Marpole and Gulf of Georgia. These two groups follow the general separation initially noted by Hill-Tout (1895), Smith (1903) and Drucker (1943) as much as a century earlier.

In consort with the idea of a population replacement, Burley adds a complex feedback explanation for the Marpole transition (see Figure 3.1).

Burley envisions the pre-Marpole people as generalized hunter-gatherers grouped in small mobile egalitarian bands (1980, 1983). He believes these people, represented by the Locarno skeletal population and Locarno Beach toolkit, lived in the Gulf of Georgia region subsisting on a diversified coastal resource base.

Contemporaneously in the Fraser River Canyon where resources were limited to land mammals and anadromous fish, the ancestors of Burley and Beattie's (1987) Salish population developed more specialized artifact industries for a more specific resource base (Burley 1980,1983). Burley (1983) cites data from Mitchell (1971b) and Matthewes (1973) of a decreased availability of land mammals in the region around 3000 BP due to climatic change. According to Burley (1983), this caused a further specialization on salmon procurement in the Fraser River Canyon. The technology of salmon storage had been previously developed (Schalk 1977, Croes and Hackenberger 1988, Matson 1992) and was at this time intensified in the face of economic necessity.

This intensification was hypothesized to have happened where the Fraser River first narrows, near present day Hope/Yale (Burley 1980,1983). Burley (1980, 1983) believes the canyon gave rise to increased

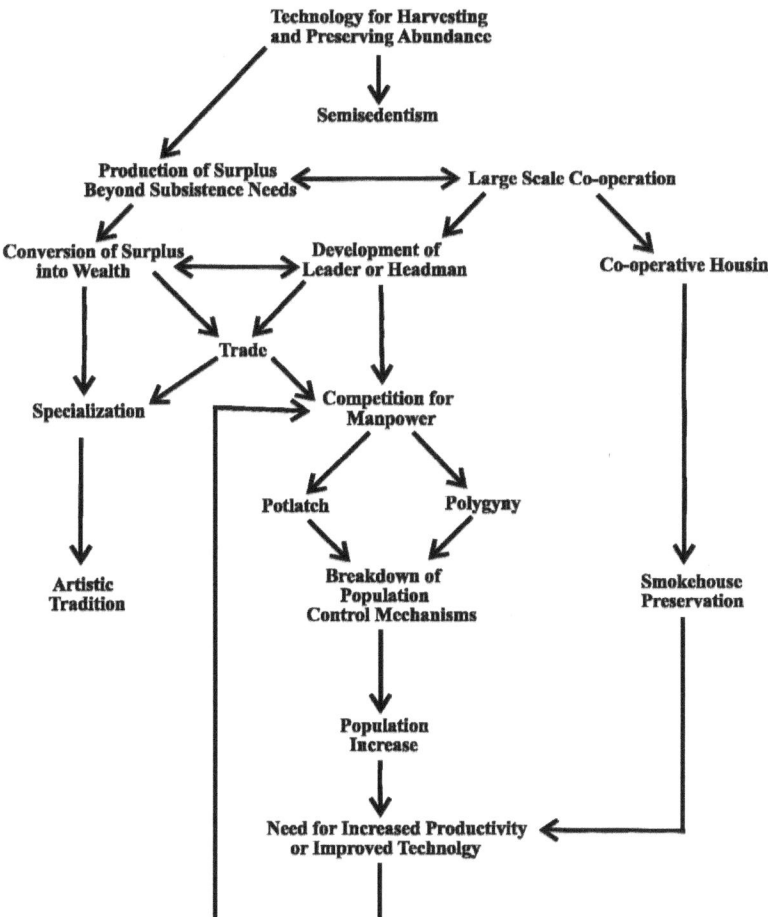

Figure 3.1 Development of the Gulf of Georgia Variant of the Northwest Coast Cultural Pattern.
After: Burley 1983:169.

resource specialization prior to the Gulf of Georgia for three reasons:

First, as previously mentioned, the Fraser River Canyon had a more specific resource base than the Gulf of Georgia, leaving canyon populations with fewer economic alternatives in times of resource stress. Where the peoples of the Gulf of Georgia had the choice of marine and foreshore fauna to even out cyclical fluctuations of other resources, canyon dwellers had only one option, salmon intensification[1].

Second, Burley (1980) notes that salmon procurement in the Fraser River Canyon is technologically less complex than its coastal counterpart. The concentration of salmon in the river canyon allows for a simpler technology of exploitation. Dip nets are all that are needed to catch salmon in the backeddies and resting pools of the Fraser River Canyon. Coastal adaptation of the salmon fishery required the development of complex composite technology and the cooperation and organization of a large labour force. Stone weirs and reef-netting, two extraction techniques employed in the Gulf of Georgia, require considerably more technological and labour investment than does dip netting (Schalk 1977, Kew 1992). From this Burley argues the simpler form is most likely the ancestral, a sentiment echoed by Kew (1992).

Third, as noted by many archaeologists from Hill-Tout (1895, 1903, 1904, 1905, 1907, 1948) and Smith (1907, 1929) to Borden (1950, 1951, 1958, 1960) and Burley (1980, 1983) the Marpole assemblage has a distinctive interior appearance and has key differences with the preceding Locarno Beach. Thin faceted ground slate knives and changes in projectile point style are implicated as of Plateau origin (Burley 1980). Burley and Beattie (1987) note the affiliation of thin ground slate knives in the much older Eayem phase in the Fraser Canyon. The authors also argue that projectile points vary considerably from a majority of ground stone forms in Locarno Beach to mostly chipped stone varieties in Marpole. Also, changes in harpoon style, the authors argue, indicate a population replacement. The composite toggling harpoons of Locarno Beach are replaced with unilaterally barbed varieties. Burley and Beattie (1987) see this as a shift to a more fragile and less efficient technology, a situation not easily explained using continuity. The authors argue that continuity should show the increased refinement and efficiency of technology which is not occurring.

Burley incorporates this idea of a population replacement into his explanation for the development of the Northwest Coast cultural pattern (see Figure 3.1). Burley's (1980, 1983) explanation is independent of the Marpole transition, however it is clear that he views the transition as the period when the Northwest Coast cultural pattern develops. Burley (1980, 1983) operates on the assumption of this population replacement and the processes depicted in Figure 3.1, apply to the new settler population. In this explanation, Burley (1980, 1983) sees salmon storage technology as a necessary preexisting condition (Schalk 1977).

The impetus for change would be a new population from the Fraser River Canyon settling on the coast and overtaxing the carrying capacity in the Gulf of Georgia. This new group, having already adapted a specialized resource strategy from the canyon, employed this new technique at the mouth of the Fraser River. Their technology of extraction needed to be adapted to new conditions and the organization of labour needed to be expanded, thus Burley (1980, 1983) suggests the development of headmen to fill the role of labour organizers.

Once this feedback loop described by Burley (1980, 1983) begins in motion, competition for labour and population increase serve to accelerate the rate of change. Small status inequalities present in pre-Marpole populations are magnified as the resource owning elite become disassociated from the labouring class. This process is compounded over time as ever increasing surpluses are appropriated by the elite and used to reinforce their prestige over others via trade and potlatching.

The discontinuity explanations have, for the most part, themselves been replaced by more generally accepted explanations of continuity. The early skeletal evidence of Hill-Tout (1895) and Drucker (1929) was rejected as unscientific and ignorant of cultural cranial deformation practices. The newer osteological evidence of Burley and Beattie (1987) has not been universally accepted as conclusive (Matson 1989, Mitchell pers. comm.). In addition, Curtin's (1999) work on Gabriola Island has shown evidence for continuity in skeletal assemblages. Burley's explanation although significantly more developed than previous discontinuity explanations, is still rife with speculation. A number of key assumptions, if found to be false, would nullify his migration explanation. The processes explained by Burley (Figure 3.1), may have operated independently of a population movement. Although Burley (1980, 1983) applies

---

[1] As mentioned in Chapter Two the contribution of plants to prehistoric diets is unknown. This explanation and several others argue for changes in subsistence but neglect the use of plant resources in their subsistence reconstructions. This undermines the credibility of such explanations of culture change based on subsistence reorganization. See Peacock 1998.

Figure 3.1 to his settler population, it may have equally affected any *in situ* population.

The major differences that appeared to exist in the artifact assemblages of Locarno Beach and Marpole have been lessened with the identification of Matson et al.'s (1980) subphases of Marpole. The subphases provide an empirical basis for a continuous in situ development of the Gulf of Georgia cultural sequence as proposed by Mitchell (1971b). Statistical support for internal evolution from Locarno Beach through Marpole to the Gulf of Georgia culture type has been widely accepted (Matson et al. 1980, Matson and Coupland 1995, Mitchell 1990, Carlson 1990a). When viewed subjectively, the artifact assemblage, much like the osteological evidence, offers a perception of difference. Many researchers have focused on the importance of that perceived difference and argued that only discontinuity can account for the apparent change. Discontinuity is contingent on a pronounced shift in technology at the Locarno Beach - Marpole interface; if that shift is not dramatic then discontinuity is controvertible.

The applicability of dislocation explanations will be revisited in Chapter Seven. In light of new evidence provided by this thesis, discontinuity may prove more likely than currently thought.

Continuity Explanations

The second set of explanations favours continuity and also has a long standing basis in the Gulf of Georgia. The works of Boas (1889, 1890, 1894, 1909) and Kroeber (1939) concentrated on in situ development of traditional cultures. Donald Mitchell (1971b, 1990) has been a staunch proponent of the continuity explanation for culture change in the Gulf of Georgia. Rather than focusing on change in the archaeological record, Mitchell looked at continuities between Locarno Beach and Marpole. He found contracting stem chipped stone points, large leaf shaped chipped stone points, microblades, faceted ground slate knives, labrets, earspools and grooved or notched sinker stones in both culture types (Mitchell 1971b). Matson (1989:9) furthers the point by stating that artifact types unique to Locarno Beach are often rare "and little difference in the abundance of common artifacts actually appears to be present between Locarno [Beach] and the later Marpole material".

Mitchell (1971b) also examined skeletal and ethnographic data and found no evidence in osteology or oral history to support a population replacement during the Marpole transition. On the contrary, linguistic evidence points to a long established presence of Salish in the Gulf of Georgia region (Mitchell 1971b, Suttles and Elmendorf 1962, Jorgensen 1969). In addition, ethnographic Coast Salish lacked the militaristic organization needed if they had been the aggressors in a population replacement (Mitchell 1971b).

Based on strong evidence and a clear argument, Mitchell's (1971b, 1990) views have won favour with virtually all Northwest Coast archaeologists. There is also statistical support for continuity; Matson (1974 and Matson et al. 1980) used multidimensional scaling analysis in his studies and concludes that continuity best explains the Locarno Beach - Marpole transition, although he notes that the possibility of population migration has not been completely ruled out (Matson 1989).

Whereas discontinuity views change as the result of population movement, here the change is the production of in situ adaptation to changing ecological factors. There is much debate in the archaeological community as to the varying importance of these factors as each researcher looks for a prime mover. Climate change, technology, social organization and conflict have all been implicated as the impetus for the Marpole transition (see Table 3.1).

When Mitchell (1971b), conceived of the change from Locarno Beach to Marpole he saw the shift as a product of climate change. He felt changing climate caused a reorientation of society to best exploit a changing resource base. Locarno Beach was focused on a generalized resource base, with sea and land mammal important, as evident in the artifact assemblage and site distribution. Locarno Beach sites were centred on the Gulf Islands and possessed a generalized toolkit (see Chapter Two). Marpole marked a shift away from the Gulf Islands and in the direction of the Fraser River. This move coincided with the replacement of a generalized subsistence strategy with a more specialized strategy based on salmon (Mitchell 1971b).

Mitchell (1971b) felt that a cooling climate lead to a decrease in oak and camas. Deer and wapiti population were also adversely affected. This produced a significant disruption to the generalized subsistence strategy being employed during Locarno Beach. Marpole reflects the intensification on salmon as a coping mechanism to deal with resource stress (Mitchell 1971b).

Croes and Hackenberger (1988) offer a different explanation based on resource depletion derived from the principles of Human Evolutionary Ecology. Building on previous work (Croes 1987, see Chapter Two for a discussion), Croes and Hackenberger (1988) see Locarno Beach and Marpole as economic plateaus and the interface between them as a technological adaptation which caused rapid change (see Figure 2.2).

Archaeologist	Reference	Prime Mover	Result
Mitchell	1971b	Climate change	Cooling climate during postglacial leads to decreased oak, camas, deer and wapiti. Forced reliance on other resources. Salmon harvesting becomes intensified.
Croes and Hackenberger	1988	Technological adaptation to resource depletion	Population pressure at the end of Locarno Beach over-tapped carrying capacity for winter shellfish exploitation. Depletion of resource base leads to development of storage technology to overcome this inadequacy. Intensification and specialization on salmon storage the result.
Matson	1983, 1989	Resource ownership	The most reliable and abundant resources become owned. Sedentism develops to enforce ownership rights. Over time, differential hereditary access to resources creates inequality.
Coupland	1985	Restriction of access to resources	Group ownership of predictable resources occurs. Sedentism for resource defense develops. Resource specialization for economic efficiency follows. Competition for labour control and surplus production selects for leaders. Internal ranking arises as a positive feedback loop as household size increases.
Hayden	1994, 1995	Competitive feasts	Wealthy individuals hold competitive feasts in which they give gifts and food; in return they receive the promise of future repayment. The wealthy collect their debts via labour during salmon season in order to generate larger surpluses. Surpluses are used to hold more grandiose competitive feasts.
Ames	1983	Hierarchical information flow	Territory becomes circumscribed by increasing population. Once resilient systems become constrained. Hierarchical information flow provides more efficient monitoring of cultural and environmental shifts. Ranking develops as a stable response for adaptation.
Mitchell	1989	Circumscription, conflict	Territorial expansion of neighbouring groups forces the development of internal sociocultural complexity. This complexity is expressed archaeologically as Marpole.

Table 3.1 Continuity Explanations

The authors believe that Locarno Beach represents a generalized seasonal procurement strategy. Sea and land mammal, fresh fish, shellfish, and plants make up the majority of the diet (Croes and Hackenberger 1988). In addition, Croes and Hackenberger (1988) believe that storage of flatfish is also occurring and foreshadows the development of salmon storage in Marpole. They hypothesize that during Locarno Beach population growth outstrips carrying capacity, particularly in winter, where shellfish gathering is the limiting factor (Croes and Hackenberger 1988). Over-collecting of shellfish would serve to decrease the shellfish population's ability to recover, thus further depleting the resource. Croes and Hackenberger (1988) believe an economic shift was made to specialize on salmon storage to overcome seasonal food shortages. The technology of fish storage was in place during Locarno Beach but was not intensive (Matson 1992, Pratt 1992). Economic necessity forced its increased use in Marpole.

Mitchell (1971b) and Croes and Hackenberger (1988) believe Marpole is the archaeological expression of the shift to stored salmon as a primary resource. They see a salmon storage economy as vital to the production of surplus, the development of sedentism, and the evolution of hereditary status inequality. The next few authors I will discuss focus on the rise of status inequality after the storage of salmon had been developed. Several of these explanations are meant as general models for the rise of status inequality on the Northwest Coast. When applied to the Gulf of Georgia region, these models become explanations for the Locarno Beach - Marpole transition, as this is the period in which the hallmarks of ascribed status inequality develop. I will discuss each explanation with regards to the Marpole transition but the implications of the author's models may be broader reaching than I describe.

Matson (1983, 1985, 1989, 1992) saw the prime mover for the Marpole transition as resource ownership, asserting that due to circumscription, abundant and predictable resources became owned. He feels that for ownership to occur there must be worthwhile dividends. The investment of ownership, i.e. defense of owned resources, will only initially be profitable in abundant and predicable resources. As the system becomes more circumscribed, lesser quality resources will be incorporated into owned territory. In other words the more competition for resources, the more ownership of resource areas should be expected. Matson (1983, 1989, 1992) notes that salmon procurement zones should be the first owned resource areas as they are the most abundant and predictable. Sedentism develops as a territorial defense technique to protect ownership rights. Matson (1983, 1989, 1992) also believes that ownership of salmon fishing locations coupled with sedentism led to specialization of salmon harvesting. He feels that with increased reliance on the salmon harvesting more efficient technology would develop to better exploit the fishery. Familiarity breeds efficiency. Matson (1983, 1989, 1992) uses this logic to explain the thin ground slate knife industry as adaptive for salmon processing. Burley (1980, 1983), on the other hand invokes this as evidence of dislocation.

Matson (1992, n.d.) has shown that intensive salmon storage predates the Marpole transition at at least one site, Crescent Beach. Given that the technology to intensively exploit salmon is not directly related to the Marpole assemblage, the meaning of Marpole is questioned. Mitchell (1971b, 1990) and Croes and Hackenberger (1988) see the Marpole culture type as the product of intensive salmon exploitation. Matson (1992) feels that Marpole represents increased efficiency in the exploitation of salmon resources. This efficiency was gained through familiarity with the intensive salmon harvesting garnered through resource ownership induced sedentism.

The Deviation Amplifying Model of the Evolution of Status Inequality (Figure 3.2), shows Coupland's (1985) explanation for the Marpole Transition. In his explanation, Coupland (1985) follows similar lines of reasoning as does Matson (1983, 1989, 1992) shown above. Coupland (1985) sees restriction of access to resources as the prime mover much like Matson's (1983,1989,1992) resource ownership explanation.

Coupland (1985) believes successive restrictions in access cause further intensification in the processes of status inequality development. Unlike Matson's (1983,1989, 1992) explanation where successive stages of resources become owned, from high quality abundant and predictable resources to lower quality, more patchy ones, Coupland's (1985) explanation sees successive constriction of ownership groups, from extended family through to individual leader.

The Deviation-Amplifying Model shows the progression of access restriction stages, each stage causing further changes in the social system. Resource specialization, sedentism and cooperative housing are outcomes of initial restrictions (Coupland 1985).

The second narrowing of the corporate group intensifies this process by creating competition for labour, wealth and prestige (Coupland 1985). The last stage sees the institution of hereditary wealthy sociopolitical elites (Coupland 1985).

Coupland (1985) argues that his explanation based on deviation-amplification or positive feedback differs from others that are based on negative feedback. Resource depletion explanations are based on the inverse relationship between resource availability and status inequality. Coupland's (1985) explanation looks at the positive link between increasing restriction of access to resources and increasing status inequality.

Brian Hayden (1994, 1995) offers a completely different explanation for the development of Northwest Coast sociocultural complexity. Hayden (1994, 1995) developed his explanation to suit Plateau prehistory but readily exports his findings to the coast and more generally to complex hunter-gatherers everywhere. For Hayden (1994, 1995) the prime mover behind the rise of status inequality is more personal. Competitive feasts are an arena to showcase prestige and create social obligations (Hayden 1994, 1995). These competitive feasts, known ethnographically on the Northwest Coast as potlatches, involve individuals distributing gifts and food in lavish displays of wealth (Boas 1894).

Hayden (1994, 1995) believes that through the potlatch individuals could exchange wealth for social obligations that must be repaid in future. These debts could be collected via labour during salmon harvesting season. This would allow the wealthy to generate an even larger surplus. Hayden (1994, 1995) feels this surplus would be reinvested in potlatching to raise individual prestige and create further social debts. A feedback mechanism develops whereby the wealthy get wealthier and the poor become labour which is increasingly in demand. Thus, small initial differences in wealth and prestige occurring

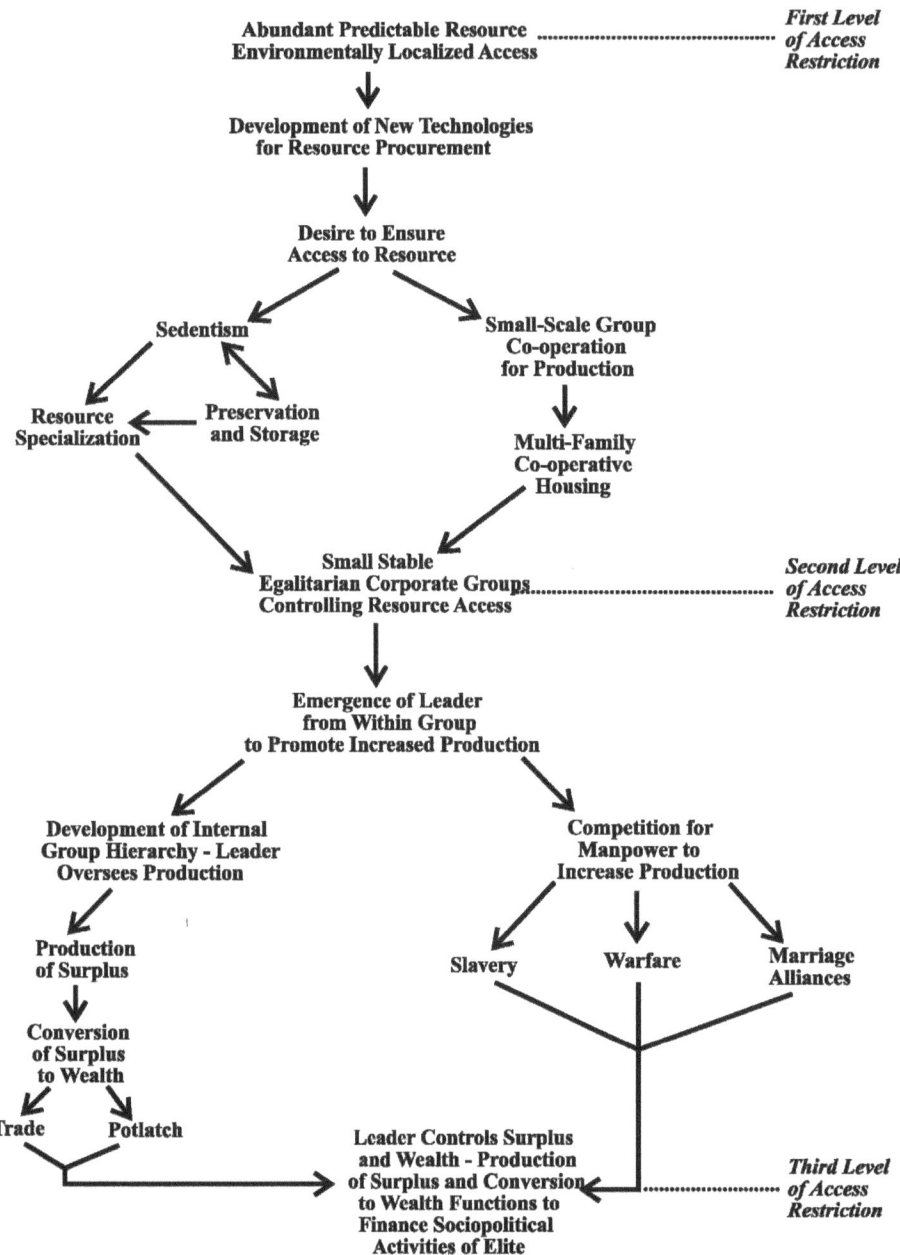

Figure 3.2 Deviation-Amplifying Model of the Evolution of Status Inequality, The Northwest Coast Example.
After: Coupland 1985:224

as a whole, his explanation can be related directly to the Marpole transition.

Ames (1983) defines foraging societies as resilient systems. That is, the generalized nature of subsistence and social interaction allows for a great deal of flexibility in adaptation (Ames 1983). In the Gulf of Georgia, where population increased during Locarno Beach and became circumscribed, the resiliency of the system was lost. The ability of the system to adapt became limited to internal mechanisms (Ames 1983). One means of internal adaptation is ranking. Ames (1983) feels ranking was chosen because of the efficiency of hierarchical information flow. Ranking allows for rapid response to environmental and cultural changes through vertical dissemination of knowledge. Thus, changes in resource availability are more efficiently coped with when fewer high ranking individuals making communal decisions.

Along a similar vein, Mitchell (1989) proposes that circumscription is the driving force behind the development of Marpole. Unlike Ames (1983,1985) however, Mitchell (1989) looks to external rather than internal stimuli for the Marpole transition. Based on his work in the Queen Charlotte Strait, Mitchell (1989) discovered evidence for Wakashan territorial expansion between 2500 and 2000 BP. To the West, Nuu-chah-nulth speakers may have also been making inroads into the area (McMillan 1998). Mitchell (1989, 1990) feels Marpole may be a response to this external threat of territorial expansion of neighboring groups. This follows the logic of Carneiro's (1970)

during Locarno Beach were amplified in Marpole through individual competition.

Kenneth Ames (1979, 1981, 1983, 1985, 1995) developed a general model of ranking among foraging groups. The model looks to define the process by which ranking evolves in hunter-gatherer populations worldwide. Ames (1983) applies his model to the Northwest Coast and more specifically the Gulf of Georgia. Although intended for the evolution of ranking

Circumscription Theory. Internal complexity can arise in reaction to external pressure.

The continuity explanations have focused on in situ development across the Locarno Beach - Marpole interface. As has been presented, each researcher has a different viewpoint on the prime mover which explains the transition. These explanations are rife with speculation and the archaeological implications of each explanation are difficult to test. This gives very little ability to chose between them and at this point I will not.

I currently favour a synthetic explanation which sees inadequate resource availability, whether produced by resource depletion, population growth, unequal access to resources or other phenomena stimulating an intensified reliance on the salmon fishery. Exploitation of other resources cannot be readily intensified. Croes and Hackenberger (1988) believe that an intensification of the winter shellfish industry may have been attempted but instead produced resource depletion as shellfish stocks were over-collected and could not recover. Anadromous fish resources are the only ones that can be intensified without damage to the future of the resource (Matson 1989, Schalk 1977). This intensification of the salmon fishery led to a large production surplus. By some mechanism, perhaps ownership, obligation or access restriction, this surplus was not available to all members of society. Status inequities grew as the wealthy reinvested the surplus through trade and potlatching. The power of the elite was stabilized by marriage alliance and warfare. This series of interconnected processes is expressed archaeologically as the shift from Locarno Beach to Marpole.

Continuity as an explanation of the Marpole transition will be revisited in subsequent chapters. This thesis provides more fodder for the theoretical discussion of the transition and will be discussed further in Chapter Seven.

Summary
This chapter has summarized several of the explanations for the Locarno Beach - Marpole transition. Two general schools of thought have been traced, one which looks at dislocation and the other at continuity. Based on current evidence and the consensus of opinion (Burley 1980, Matson 1989, Mitchell 1990, Matson and Coupland 1995), continuity is favoured. Dislocation requires an abrupt assemblage change at the Locarno Beach - Marpole interface. Using Matson et al.'s (1980) subphases of Marpole there is not an abrupt shift. The Old Musqueam subphase is actually very difficult to distinguish from Locarno Beach assemblages (Matson and Coupland 1995). In the absence of a dramatic shift at the Locarno Beach - Marpole interface, it becomes possible to accept continuity for the time being, though this will be re-evaluated in Chapter Seven.

This chapter has dealt with general explanations of culture change for the Gulf of Georgia regional sequence. As previously mentioned, evidence from several Southern Vancouver Island sites is not entirely in agreement with the regional sequence. On Southern Vancouver Island there appear to be Locarno Beach assemblages associated with Marpole dates. The next chapter places Southern Vancouver Island within the existing culture historical framework to evaluate the applicability of these general explanations in regard to that area.

CHAPTER 4. SOUTHERN VANCOUVER ISLAND AND EXPLANATIONS OF CULTURE CHANGE

Chapter Two outlined the Gulf of Georgia culture historical sequence and the units to which it applies. Chapter Three, reviewed explanations of the shift from one unit to another, Locarno Beach to Marpole. This chapter places Southern Vancouver Island in the context of the aforementioned explanations. A discussion of the suitability of the regional culture historical sequence for depicting the Marpole transition on Southern Vancouver Island follows. Arising from this discussion, the thesis question is developed and the multiple working hypotheses are examined.

The idea for this thesis began with my work at Kosapsom with the University of Victoria Archaeological Field School. Three seasons of excavation produced two prehistoric components, one apparently assignable to the Gulf of Georgia culture type and one to Locarno Beach. Radiocarbon analysis was not however in agreement with this interpretation. C^{14} dates were well within the accepted range of Marpole with only one date clearly associated with Locarno Beach (see Table A1.1). Conversations with Mitchell (pers. comm.) and Keddie (pers. comm.) lead me to believe that Marpole may be absent entirely from Southern Vancouver Island. Examining site reports from Willows Beach (Kenny 1974) and Quick's Pond (Clark 1984) it became apparent that there was some ambiguity as to the nature of Marpole on Southern Vancouver Island. These sites had assemblages with characteristics from both Locarno Beach and Marpole. Kenny (1974) and Clark (1984) noted difficulty in interpreting these sites because of ambiguous assemblages.

Returning to the culture historical sequence (see Figure 2.1) which sees a transition from Locarno Beach to Marpole at 2500/2400 BP, I began to think that the transition on Southern Vancouver Island was somewhat more complicated than the sequence allowed. Some researchers (Mitchell pers. comm., Keddie pers. comm.) felt there may be no Marpole on Southern Vancouver Island at all. Radiocarbon dates place seemingly Locarno Beach assemblages within the accepted date range of Marpole (Mackie pers. comm.). Other sites (Kenny 1974, Clark 1984) had traits of both culture types present. Yet there had been no real challenge of the utility of the Gulf-wide culture historical sequence. This thesis is meant to fill that void.

The current state of knowledge on Southern Vancouver Island is such that wholesale acceptance of the regional sequence has created three distinct problems. First, sites without associated radiocarbon dates have been defined as Locarno Beach based on the assemblages. As is seen in the Kosapsom material, some Locarno Beach assemblages are associated with Marpole dates. Without the benefit of radiocarbon analysis the site age for Kosapsom would have been estimated to between 3500/3300 to 2500/2400 BP. This contrasts with the C^{14} dates which place the site between 2770 ± 50 and 1960 ± 50 BP (see Table A1.1). This process serves to inflate site age at some sites on Southern Vancouver Island. Thus other Locarno Beach sites without the assistance of 14C age estimates have the potential for being younger than currently thought.

Second, some sites with radiocarbon dates within the range of Marpole have been assigned to Marpole without regard to the assemblage composition (Mitchell pers. comm.). When in doubt archaeologists refer to the standard reference, the culture historical sequence. If a site is dated to Marpole then it must be Marpole. There is no room in the regional sequence for any other interpretation. Thus Marpole may be over-represented on Southern Vancouver Island. Sites with Marpole-age C^{14} dates may be associated with Locarno Beach or some other archaeological unit, yet are interpreted as Marpole based solely on the regional sequence.

Third, some sites on Southern Vancouver Island have mixed assemblages but have been interpreted more simply to fit the culture historical sequence. For example, Quick's Pond has moderately more Locarno Beach attributes than Marpole traits. The decision to assign Quick's Pond to the Locarno Beach culture type was simply based on a count of assignable attributes, Locarno Beach had eleven present while Marpole had only ten (Clark 1984). The field of Northwest Coast archaeology accepts the interpretation of Quick's Pond as Locarno Beach without major reservation. A complex site is made very simple, thus some incongruities within the regional sequence have become masked.

These problems revolve around the inability of the current regional sequence to depict the culture history of Southern Vancouver Island. There appears to be a number of sites where the regional sequence fails to adequately explain the variation seen on Southern Vancouver Island. Therein lies the purpose of this thesis, to resolve ambiguity seen in the Southern Vancouver Island assemblages during the Marpole transition and give another interpretive choice to archaeologists when defining these assemblages.

I believe there is sufficient reason to re-examine the accepted regional culture sequence for Southern Vancouver Island. The development of Marpole on Southern Vancouver Island apparently does not mirror that on the Fraser River. The question of how Southern Vancouver Island differs and why is integral to this thesis.

Can the shift from Locarno Beach to Marpole (2600-1500 BP) on Southern Vancouver Island be explained in terms of the existing culture historical framework? This question will be evaluated against three working hypotheses. These hypotheses are attempts by archaeologists to explain the variation found on Southern Vancouver Island during the Locarno Beach - Marpole transition.

The first working hypothesis is that the Old Musqueam subphase of Marpole begins in the Fraser River and takes time to diffuse to the islands. Matson and Coupland (1995) argue that Marpole is a Fraser River adaptation and the incipience of Marpole should be found there. The first Marpole subphase, Old Musqueam, is known from five sites, all but one of which are mainland sites. The sole exception is Fossil Bay on Sucia Island in the San Juan Islands. Matson and Coupland (1995) interpret this pattern as evidence for their notion of a Fraser River "birthplace" for Marpole.

If this is the case, my results should show a later date of appearance of Marpole on Southern Vancouver Island. The absence of the Old Musqueam subphase, with Marpole's first incarnation being Beach Grove subphase or Old Musqueam's later dating on the island would provide support for this theory. If my results confirm this idea then this thesis will make specific the dating of the inception of Marpole on Southern Vancouver Island and trace the development of Marpole geographically across the Gulf of Georgia.

The second working hypothesis is that the initial interpretations that gave rise to this study were inaccurate. The earlier assemblages found at Kosapsom, may in fact be representative of the Old Musqueam subphase of Marpole and not Locarno Beach as thought. Matson notes the similarity between Locarno Beach and Old Musqueam assemblages and the difficulty separating the two (Matson and Coupland 1995). Given this difficulty and the potential lack of experience of archaeologists in employing Matson's (1980) subphases of Marpole it becomes possible that Old Musqueam assemblages are being misinterpreted as Locarno Beach.

In this case, I would predict that multidimensional scaling would show that the Southern Vancouver Island assemblages would plot more closely with the Old Musqueam sites as defined by Matson and Coupland (1995:211-217) than with Locarno Beach assemblages. If this does turn out to be the case, the regional sequence would then be revised to allow for a Marpole culture type on Southern Vancouver Island as old as that found on the mainland. This hypothesis is incompatible with the preceding one, which states Old Musqueam is a Fraser River phenomenon exclusively.

The first two hypotheses fit within the current cultural historical sequence. As noted in Chapter Two, culture types are based on formal similarities exclusive of time and space. Therefore, if the result of this thesis is that the geographic or temporal boundaries of the culture types are amended, this amounts to a simple revision rather than a more comprehensive reworking of the regional sequence.

The third working hypothesis is a more substantial challenge to the culture sequence. This hypothesis, favoured by Grant Keddie (pers. comm.) and Donald Mitchell (pers. comm.) is that Marpole did not exist on Southern Vancouver Island. If the Old Musqueam subphase is defined as very Locarno Beach-like and the Garrison subphase is equally Gulf of Georgia-like, with the defining characteristics being vague, it may be possible that Old Musqueam is properly assigned to Locarno Beach and Garrison to Gulf of Georgia. Marpole proper may then be seen as only the Beach Grove subphase. It has been argued (Keddie, pers. comm.) that the Beach Grove subphase is the most Fraser River centered of the subphases and does not exist as defined elsewhere. If the Southern Vancouver Island data support this hypothesis, then the question of what replaces Marpole on Southern Vancouver Island between 2500/2400 and 1500/1100 BP?, must be answered. Analysis may show late Locarno Beach dates and the absence of any assemblage that can be characterized as Marpole or the presence of an entirely new archaeological unit on Southern Vancouver Island.

It is also possible that none of these three hypotheses are supported by the data. If any new hypotheses arise during data analysis they will be discussed and evaluated in Chapter Six.

The Locarno Beach - Marpole transition is a critical time period in the development of the hallmarks of historically and ethnographically documented Northwest Coast cultures. Marpole sees the rise and intensification of food storage, status inequality, longhouses and an elaborate artistic sphere, all characteristic of contact period Northwest Coast cultures. The Marpole culture type has been seen as an important step towards the evolution of sociocultural complexity (Ames 1983, 1985, 1995, Croes 1987, 1988, Matson and Coupland 1995, see Chapter Three)

The development of sociocultural complexity within a foraging group has always sat uneasily in anthropologists' simple models of social organization and subsistence (such as Morgan 1877, Service 1962, Sahlins

1963, White 1959, Steward 1955 and Fried 1967, among others). A better understanding of the process of increasing sociocultural complexity will serve to broaden knowledge in Northwest Coast prehistory but also in Anthropology as a discipline. An understanding of this knowledge is even more important given that there is a very real possibility that one part of a region (Fraser River) adopts intensive resource extraction and develops more markers of status differentiation several hundred years prior to another area within the same region (Southern Vancouver Island). These two areas are linked in culture history, geography, and language, yet may have differing trajectories towards social stratification. Given this backdrop, this study will hopefully illuminate the processes by which sociocultural complexity arises.

Although some minor faults have been apparent in the Gulf of Georgia regional sequence for years, no one has really questioned its essential validity. This project accepts the cultural historical sequence of the Gulf of Georgia and does not question it wholesale. During a specific time period (2600-1500 BP) and for a specific area (Southern Vancouver Island), the sequence is re-examined in an attempt to make the sequence more accurate, not rewrite it.

The next chapter reviews how this study has been undertaken. A discussion of the methods of data collection and analysis is presented. In addition, the means of testing the working hypotheses is explained. Chapters Six and Seven will offer those results and discuss some of the possible implications to the field of Northwest Coast archaeology.

CHAPTER 5. DATA SET AND ANALYSIS

The previous chapter proposed the thesis question and the three working hypotheses. This chapter explains how the thesis question is answered and how the working hypotheses are evaluated. The first half of this chapter is a definition of the data set. The study area sites analyzed in this thesis are introduced and the process of site selection is discussed. Data collection and compilation procedures are laid out. Following this, the taxonomic classification employed in this study is presented. Artifacts types are defined as they were used in data classification and problems in classification are discussed.

The second half of this chapter presents a discussion of the analytical procedures used to evaluate the working hypotheses. As mentioned previously, this thesis is an expanded replication of Matson et al.'s (1980) multidimensional scaling study. As such I also use metric multidimensional scaling as the main statistical procedure in this thesis. This chapter explains how Matson et al. (1980) used multidimensional scaling in their study. A general description of multidimensional scaling principles follows. The specific implementation of statistics in this thesis is also being presented.

Sites

In planning this thesis I chose to investigate an arbitrary study area. This was done for a variety of reasons. Most importantly, the composition and location of any emically important social units for the period 2600 - 1500 BP is unknown. Settlement type and location, seasonal site usage, subsistence pattern, and level of status differentiation all appear to change drastically between the time of the Locarno Beach culture type and that of the ethnographically known Gulf of Georgia cultures. It is safe to say, within this milieu of change, social organization was also affected to some degree.

Extrapolating current social organization and territories two millennia into the past is at best sketchy and certainly not defensible here. An arbitrary study circumvents this preconceived notion of past social structure. The use of a subjective study area could reflect researcher bias rather than valid archaeological patterns. In addition, the use of metric multidimensional scaling allows for the discovery of patterns of similarity which may be aspects of social organization. Multidimensional scaling groups site components based on commonalities between assemblages. It is left to the researcher to interpret these groups and one possible explanation is that the groupings reflect differences in social patterning.

The study area consists of two Borden units[1], DcRt and DcRu, which cover a large portion of present-day Greater Victoria. The two Borden units were chosen as they provide a well-excavated and manageable sample of archaeological sites on Southeastern Vancouver Island. Each of the nearly 300 archaeological sites within DcRt and DcRu was examined against two criteria for possible inclusion in this study.

First, the sites must be believed to be associated with the Locarno Beach - Marpole transition. Site components must be dated either by relative dating of their artifact assemblages or by radiocarbon analysis to between 2600 - 1500 BP.

This time period was chosen to represent the Locarno Beach - Marpole transition. The range begins prior to the accepted dating of the transition and continues until the earliest evidence for the shift to the Gulf of Georgia culture type.

Second, site assemblages are of a large enough sample size for analysis to occur. It is thought that a minimum of at least one hundred artifacts need to be present for a representative sample (Mitchell pers. comm.). This sample size requirement was not considered a hard and fast rule rather, it was a guideline and sites with fewer than one hundred artifacts had the potential of being included if they possessed a diverse enough sample to be statistically useful. This however turned out to be a non-issue as no potential sites had between fifty and one hundred artifacts.

---

[1] The Borden Site Designation System (Borden 1952) provides a uniform system for labeling archaeological sites in Canada. Following the National Topographic Map Series the country is divided into a grid based on latitude and longitude beginning in the Southeastern most extremity of Canada. The first two letters of the four letter Borden unit code refer to latitude. The capital letter represents two degrees of latitude while the lower case marks a subdivision of ten minutes of one degree. The next two letters depict longitude. The capital letter equates to four degrees of longitude while the lower case is representing ten minutes of one degree. This means that each Borden unit is a rectangle approximately 18 Km (North-South) and 11 Km (East-West). The study area for this thesis lies between 48° -20' and 48° -30' long. and 123° -10' and 123° -30' lat. and is approximately 400 Km^2. The number following the Borden unit is a unique site label given to a site in the order it was recorded.

This thesis began with eighteen sites but as more intense data collection began the number of sites dropped to seven. The majority of sites were dropped due to small sample size, however poor recording and too recent dating also served to disqualify site components. Maplebank, a large and important multicomponent midden site was disqualified due to its lack of analysis. The poor recording quality of the site did not allow me to separate prehistoric components in a reasonable length of time.

I was able however to separate prehistoric components at the Cadboro Bay site, which was not published. The quality of site notes and stratigraphic drawings made component separation possible (Romaine pers. comm.), this was not the case with Maplebank.

Esquimalt Lagoon was initially included in this study but was found to relate closely to the later Gulf of Georgia culture type based on assemblage composition and radiocarbon dating and was removed from the study. The sites that were chosen for this study are shown in Figure 5.1, Map of Southern Vancouver Island Study Area. The following paragraphs will introduce the study area sites.

Table 5.1 Study Area Sites
A. Northwest Cadboro Bay, DcRt 9. (NWCD) This site is one of two relatively large shell middens in Cadboro Bay. The other, DcRt 15, is also included in this study. The Northwest Cadboro Bay site extends along the beach for at least 492 metres and inland a maximum of 80 to 90 metres (Keddie 1987). A total of 101 formed artifacts were analyzed for this site. One charcoal sample has been submitted for radiocarbon dating analysis (RIDDL 571). The sample was dated to 1760 ± 110 BP (Keddie 1987). See Table 5.2, for a complete list of radiocarbon age estimates for this study.

B. Willows Beach I, DcRt 10. (WB1) Willows Beach is a large multicomponent midden site in Oak Bay. A small Gulf of Georgia culture type deposit overlies an older and larger component. Numerous excavations have been undertaken at Willows Beach (Kenny 1971, 1974, Pollit and Monks 1977, Mitchell 1986, Eldridge 1987a, 1987b, 1990, 1992a, Eldridge et al. 1991, Coates 1994, Curtin et al. 1991). Several radiocarbon age estimates are available for the older deposits, 2180 ± 70 BP (SFU 791), 2490 ± 85 BP (GaK 5103), and 2630 ± 95 BP (GaK

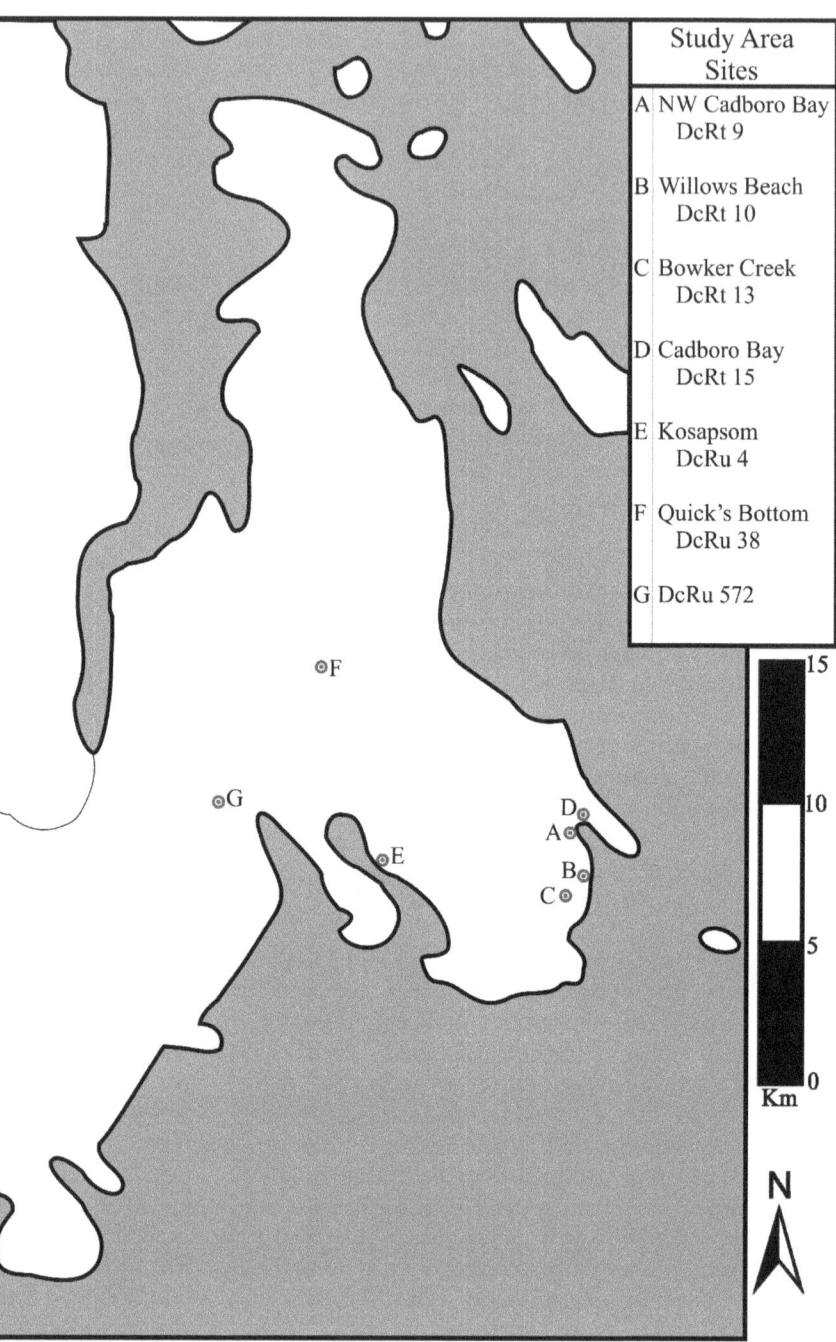

Figure 5.1 Map of Southern Vancouver Island Study Area, DcRt and DcRu.

5102) (Curtin et al. 1991). Although the oldest dates indicate a Locarno Beach age, Ray Kenny (1974) had difficulty deciding which culture type was present, Locarno Beach or Marpole, as the artifact assemblage has traits of both.

C. Bowker Creek, DcRt 13. (BC) Bowker Creek is a small but well known site located just inland from Willows Beach. The site was excavated by Donald Mitchell (1979) in 1968. Two radiocarbon age estimates of 2910 ± 100 BP (GaK 2760) and 2740 ± 100 BP (GaK 2761), place Bowker Creek firmly within Locarno Beach. This site was included in this study as it was felt there was strong likelihood that other Southern Vancouver Island sites were also of the Locarno Beach culture type and would group with Bowker Creek during the analysis. Recently however (Matson, n.d.), the dating of Bowker Creek has been called into question. The original carbon samples were taken from shell specimens. The marine reservoir effect, described in Appendix One, inflates radiocarbon age by 390 ± 23 years. Thus the age estimates for Bowker Creek are now 2520 ± 100 BP and 2350 ± 100 BP. These dates place Bowker Creek very close to the accepted Locarno Beach - Marpole transition date.

Site Component	Sample Number	Age Estimate	Material	Reference
NW Cadboro Bay	RIDDL 571	1760 ± 110	charcoal	Keddie 1987
Willows Beach I	GaK 5103	2490 ± 85	charcoal	Curtin et al.1991
Willows Beach I	GaK 5102	2630 ± 95	charcoal	Curtin et al.1991
Willows Beach I	SFU 791	2180 ± 70	charcoal	Curtin et al.1991
Bowker Creek	GaK 2761	2350 ± 100	shell	Mitchell 1979, Matson n.d.
Bowker Creek	GaK 2760	2520 ± 100	shell	Mitchell 1979, Matson n.d.
Cadboro Bay I	GaK 2751	1810 ± 90	charcoal	Wilmeth 1978
Kosapsom I	TO 5364	1960 ± 50	charcoal	Mackie, pers. comm.
Kosapsom I	CAMS 40393	2120 ± 50	charcoal	Mackie, pers. comm.
Kosapsom I	CAMS 40385	2230 ± 50	charcoal	Mackie, pers. comm.
Kosapsom I	CAMS 40394	2280 ± 50	shell	Mackie, pers. comm.
Kosapsom I	CAMS 40398	2320 ± 50	shell	Mackie, pers. comm.
Kosapsom I	TO 5365	2360 ± 60	charcoal	Mackie, pers. comm.
Kosapsom I	CAMS 40390	2450 ± 50	shell	Mackie, pers. comm.
Kosapsom I	CAMS 40386	2510 ± 50	shell	Mackie, pers. comm.
Kosapsom I	CAMS 40397	2770 ± 50	charcoal	Mackie, pers. comm.
DcRu 572	Beta 86772	2380 ± 60	shell	Owens et al. 1997

note: Radiocarbon age estimates from shell have been corrected 390 ± 23 BP, see Appendix One.

Table 5.2 Radiocarbon Age estimates for Southern Vancouver Island Site Components

D. Cadboro Bay I, DcRt 15. (CD1) The second of the two Cadboro Bay sites in this thesis, this site is northeast of DcRt 9 and is separated from it by Gyro Park. The Cadboro Bay site is large at 350 metres by 24 metres. DcRt 15, also known as Snyeqa, has a small, more recent, component overlying older deposits. Radiocarbon dating has estimated the age of the older component as 1810 ± 90 BP (GaK 2751) (Wilmeth 1978).

This site was never analyzed and published. I separated the artifact assemblage into components based on field notes and stratigraphy (Mitchell pers. comm., Romaine pers. comm.). Only those artifacts with clear association with the older Cadboro Bay I component were included in this study.

E. Kosapsom, DcRu 4. (K1) This site is on the north bank of the Gorge waterway. Kosapsom became the site of Craigflower Schoolhouse in 1853. Since that time the majority of the site has been protected as a school yard. Harlan Smith (1907) first excavated at Kosapsom a century ago. The University of Victoria Archaeological Fieldschool spent three seasons excavating at Kosapsom (Mitchell 1995, 1996, Steward n.d.). Two prehistoric components are present: one defined as Gulf of Georgia culture type and the other as Locarno Beach. Many radiocarbon dates have been analyzed for Kosapsom, 1960 ± 50 BP (TO 5364), 2120 ± 50 BP (CAMS 40393), 2230 ± 50 BP (CAMS 40385), 2280 ± 50 BP (CAMS 40394), 2320 ± 50 BP (CAMS 40398), 2360 ± 60 BP (TO 5365), 2450 ± 50 BP (CAMS 40390), 2510 ± 50 BP (CAMS 40386) and 2770 ± 50BP (CAMS 40397) (Mitchell 1996, Mackie pers. comm.). See Table 5.2 below. These majority of these dates falls within the accepted range of Marpole but the assemblages do not resemble Marpole assemblages as described elsewhere.

Quick's Pond, DcRu 38. (QP) Quick's Pond is an inland surface lithic scatter. It is the only non-shell midden site included in this thesis. This site has very little bone, only one artifact. This site has been interpreted as Locarno Beach but also has a number of Marpole traits (Clark 1984).

DcRu 572. (U572) This is one of many sites unearthed during the Vancouver Island Highway, Victoria Approaches Project (Owens et al. 1996, 1997). This large site was almost completely destroyed during highway construction. It is dated by relative dating to Locarno Beach or Marpole. Radiocarbon age estimates for the site are 2380 ± 60 (Beta 86772) which places the site very close to the Locarno Beach - Marpole interface.

Artifacts.
Matson et al. (1980) employed a standardized typology from Burley (1980) for their study. My thesis is an expanded replication of the Matson et al (1980) work and as such I will also use the Burley (1980) typology. Unfortunately, archaeological work in the Gulf of Georgia is far from standardized. The sites chosen to be included in this thesis employed a variety of classification schemes which varied from recorder to recorder. With this in mind, I undertook an extensive reclassification of all study area site components. This process, although time consuming, was meant to lessen problems of inter-observer error and provide a large, high quality data set upon which this thesis will rest. The reclassification process included the examination of over 5000 artifacts.

Definitions of the artifact types are given below. These definitions are taken from a variety of sources most notably Borden (1970), Mitchell (1971b), Matson (1974, 1976), and Burley (1980). In Northwest Coast archaeological literature there is no comprehensive list of artifact definitions, nor is there clear agreement on each artifact type. The artifact types presented are based on my interpretation of the aforementioned publications and form the classificatory scheme I employed in data collection for this thesis. There is, however, no indication of what is meant by size descriptions for several artifact types. In the case of faceted large ground stone points, which have been described as "large points with facets and are wide relative to their length" (Matson 1974:110), the means for assessing size is not discussed. Further, overlap with other categories is discussed, the class of stemless and hexagonal ground stone points are relatively narrow and "... may grade into that of faceted large points" (Matson 1974:110), but again, no differentiation criteria is given.

There is room for interpretive differences between researchers using this typology. This is one of the reasons that I chose to personally reclassify all artifacts in my study area sites. I did not however reclassify the original data from the Matson et al. (1980) study. There is a possibility that differences in classification have occurred and I will keep this in mind during my interpretation of my results.

Table 5.3 Burley's (1980) Trait List

Artifacts of Chipped Stone

Flake edge tools: any unshaped chipped stone flake that has been retouched or utilized. A broad category that accounts for virtually all miscellaneous chipped stone artifacts. See Figure 5.2, Item A.
Slate/Sandstone discs: flakes of slate or sandstone, usually bifacially flaked and used as knives. See Figure 5.2, Item B.
Pièces esquillées: chipped stone flakes or cores reduced using bipolar flaking techniques. Used as stone wedges for sectioning bone and antler. See Figure 5.2, Item C.
Microblade/core: very small and sharp blades of obsidian, quartz or other crypto-crystalline stone. Made with a specialized prepared core technology and indirect percussion. See Figure 5.2, Item D.
Chopper/chopping tools: large crudely made hand-held cobble and pebble tools, both flakes and cores, probably used for chopping. See Figure 5.2, Item E.
Corner-notch/basal-notch points: all chipped stone projectile points with notches in the corners or base. See Figure 5.2, Item F.
Leaf shaped points: chipped stone projectile points that are leaf-shaped or lenticular in plan. See Figure 5.2, Item G.
Contracting stem points: all chipped stone projectile points which have a noticeable stem which tapers towards the base. See Figure 5.2, Item H.
Expanding stem points: all chipped stone projectile points which have a noticeable stem which expands towards the base. See Figure 5.2, Item I.
Triangular points: chipped stone projectile points which appear triangular in plan. See Figure 5.2, Item J.
Formed bifacial cutting and/or scraping tools: any chipped stone flake which was created with bifacial flaking. Note: All chipped stone projectile points are also formed bifaces. In several cases, projectile points with broken or missing bases were classified as formed bifaces. See Figure 5.2, Item K.

Perforators: chipped stone flake used for drilling stone, bone, antler and shell. Usually a small flake with a pronounced point which was turned into the material being drilled. See Figure 5.2, Item L.

Artifacts of Ground Stone

Triangular points: small ground stone points, with or without facets, which are triangular in plan. See Figure 5.3, Item A.
Stemless points: all ground stone points without a stem, excluding triangular points and faceted large points. See Figure 5.3, Item B.
Stemmed points: all ground stone points with a noticeable stem, this includes all notched forms. See Figure 5.3, Item C.
Faceted large points: any large faceted ground stone point. Some of which are long and thin hexagonal points. See Figure 5.3, Item D.
Celts: ground stone cutting or chopping implement of fine grained stone. Used as adze or chisel for woodworking. See Figure 5.3, Item E.
Decorated and decorative objects: all ground stone artifacts, other than labrets, which appear to be used for decoration or personal adornment. May also be incised or pecked. See Figure 5.3, Item F.
Labrets: decorative body adornment worn to mark high status. A ground stone plug to be worn in a hole in the lower lip. Usually made of fine grained stone. See Figure 5.3, Item G.
Shaped abrasive stones: slabs of sandstone or other coarse grained stone, used like sandpaper to grind stone, bone, antler or shell artifacts. Shaped abraders have intentional edge grinding to create a desired shape. See Figure 5.3, Item H.
Irregular abrasive stones: slabs of sandstone or other coarse grained stone, used like sandpaper to grind stone, bone, antler or shell artifacts. Irregular abraders have no edge grinding or have been fragmented so no edge grinding is apparent. See Figure 5.3, Item I.
Handstones: small circular hand-held tools made of dense stone with use wear on one side. See Figure 5.3, Item J.
Stone saws: similar to abrasive stones. Made of coarse grained stone such as sandstone. Stone saws have an edge facet which is used like a saw. See Figure 5.3, Item K.

Artifacts of Pecked Stone

Hand mauls: a hand-held tool used like a hammer to pound wedges and other tools. Made of pecked stone, mauls are often large and dense to avoid breakage and often have a nipple top. See Figure 5.3, Item L.
Hammerstones: large unmodified pebbles used like hammers. Identified by the presence of edge battering. See Figure 5.3, Item M.

Perforated stones: medium to large stones with a biconical hole drilled into them. Probably used as anchors or sinker stones. See Figure 5.3, Item N.
Notched stones: similar to perforated stones in use, but instead of a perforation a notch running the circumference of the stone is the means of attachment. See Figure 5.3, Item O.
Mortar/bowls: large pecked stone slabs used as grinding mortars or hollowed out to act as containers. Bowls may be carved intricately into human or animal forms. See Figure 5.3, Item P.

Artifacts of Bone

Barbed points: ground bone points with barbs, often unilateral. Similar in shape and function to unilaterally barbed antler points but made of bone. See Figure 5.4, Item A.
Small unipoints: small ground bone points with only one pronounced point. Base may be spatulate or wedge shaped. Used for a variety of purposes including herring rakes. See Figure 5.4, Item B.
Bipoints: small ground bone points with both ends sharpened. Used for fishing. See Figure 5.4, Item C.
Mammal bone awls: Splintered or sectioned long bones shaped into awls. See Figure 5.4, Item D.
Bird bone awls: made from hollow long bones of medium and large sized birds. One end has been worked to a point and used as an awl. See Figure 5.4, Item E.
Needles: long thin pieces of bone often with a hole drilled near one end. See Figure 5.4, Item F.
Chisel/wedge tools: objects of bone that have been ground and used as a chisel or wedge. See Figure 5.4, Item G.
Ulna awls: made from the ulna of deer or elk. Distal end worked to act as an awl. See Figure 5.4, Item H.
Decorated or decorative objects: all decorated bone objects and items for personal adornment. These include pendants, figurines and beads. See Figure 5.4, Item I.
Bird bone points: any ground bone point made from the long bones of birds, may be single or bipointed. See Figure 5.4, Item J.
Bird bone tubes: made from the long bones of birds. Often edge ground to produce smooth ends. See Figure 5.4, Item K.
Incisor tools: made from rodent incisors, most often beaver. These teeth were ground and hafted and used for carving wood. See Figure 5.4, Item L.
Ground canine and other tooth pendants: decorative pendants made from the canine teeth of animals. See Figure 5.4, Item M.
Unbarbed fixed bone point: large unbarbed ground bone points not used as harpoons. See Figure 5.4, Item N.

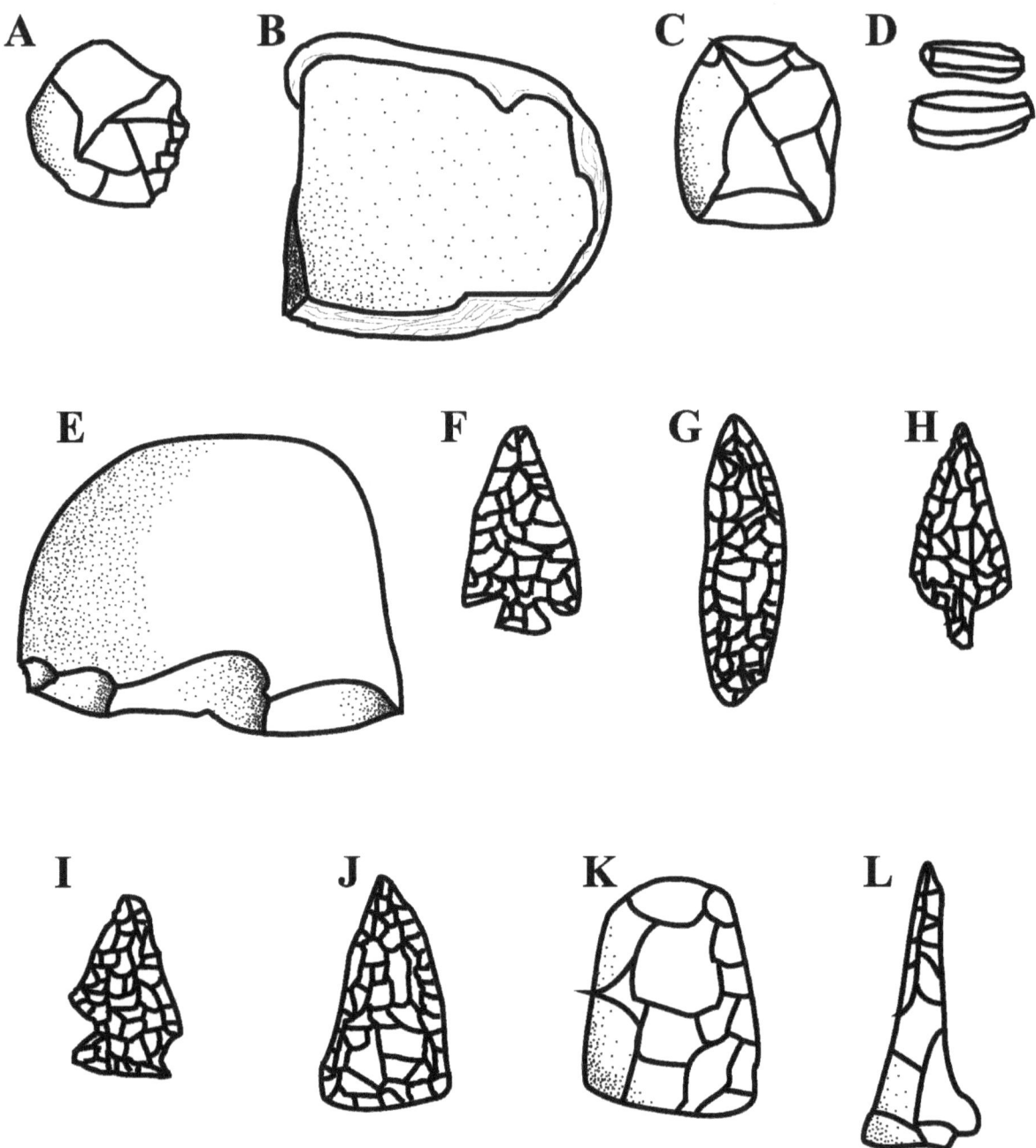

Figure 5.2 Artifacts of Chipped Stone

(A) Flake edge tool. (B) Slate/Sandstone disc. (C) Pièce esquillée. (D) Microblade/core. (E) Chopper/chopping tool. (F) Corner-notch/basal-notch point. (G) Leaf-shaped point. (H) Contracting stem point. (I) Expanding stem point. (J) Triangular point. (K) Formed bifacial cutting and/or scraping tool. (L) Perforator. Not to scale.

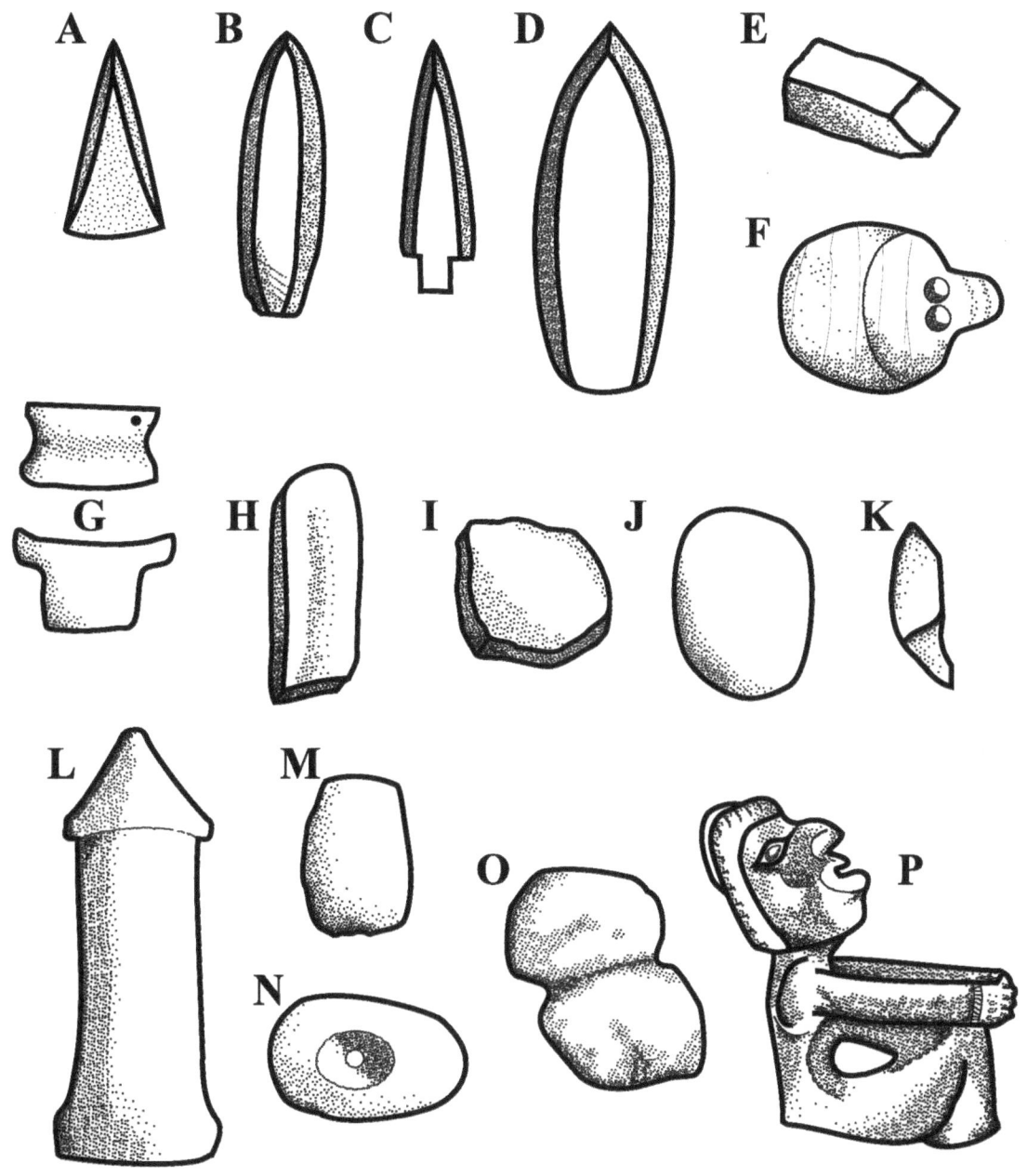

Figure 5.3 Artifacts of Ground and Pecked Stone

Ground Stone
(A) Triangular point. (B) Stemless point. (C) Stemmed point. (D) Faceted
 largepoint. (E) Celt/adze blade. (F) Decorated and decorative object.
(G) Labret.(H) Shaped abrasive stone. (I) Irregular abrasive stone.
 (J) Handstone. (K) Stone saw.

Pecked Stone
(L) Hand maul. (M) Hammerstone. (N) Perforated stone.
(O) Notched stone. (P) Mortar/bowl.
Not to scale.

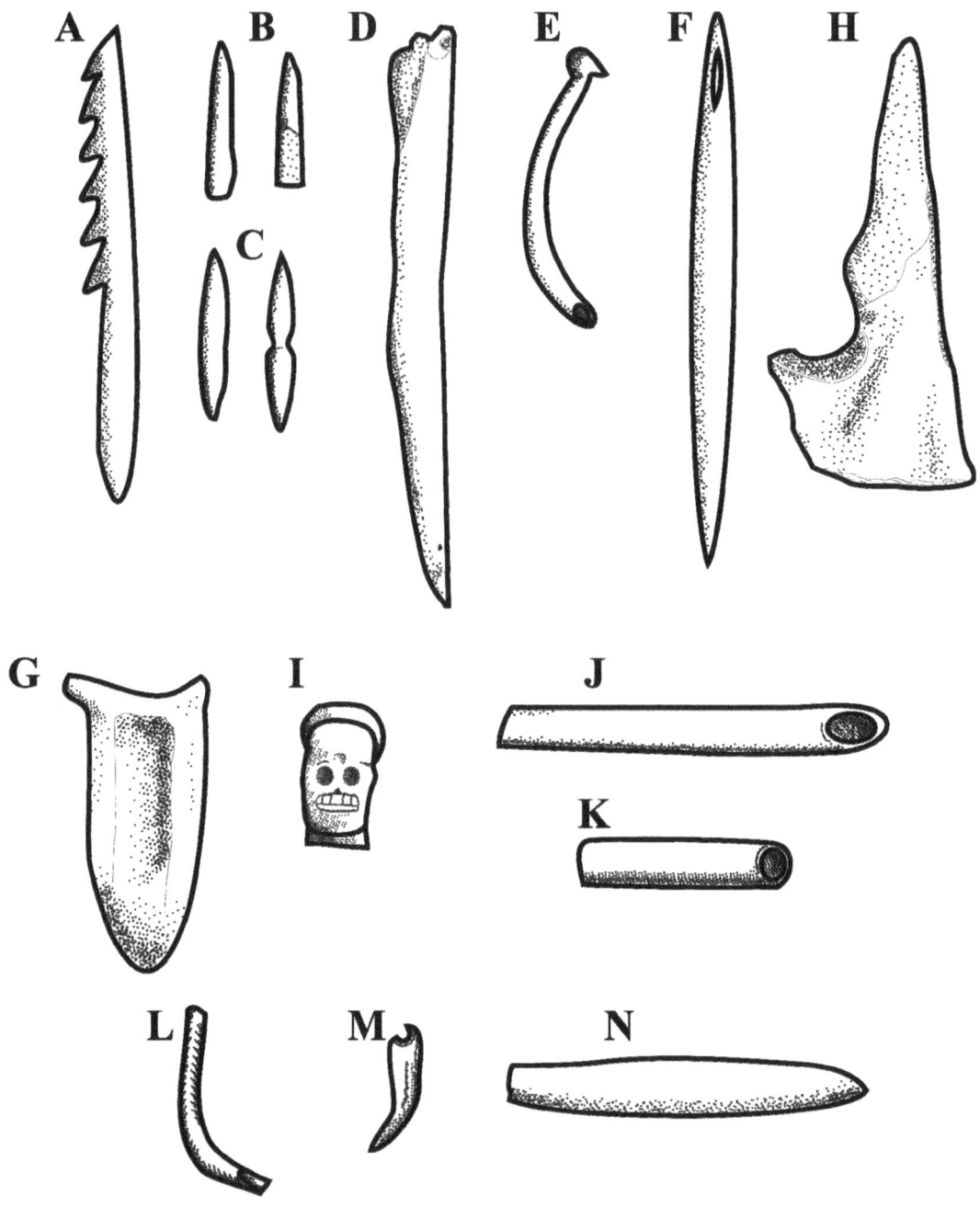

Figure 5.4 Artifacts of Bone

(A) Barbed point. (B) Small unipoints. (C) Bipoints. (D) Mammal bone awl. (E) Bird bone awl. (F) Needle. (G) Chisel/wedge tool. (H) Ulna awl. (I) Decorated or decorative object. (J) Bird bone point. (K) Bird bone tube. (L) Incisor tool. (M) Ground canine and other tooth pendant. (N) Unbarbed fixed bone point.
Not to scale.

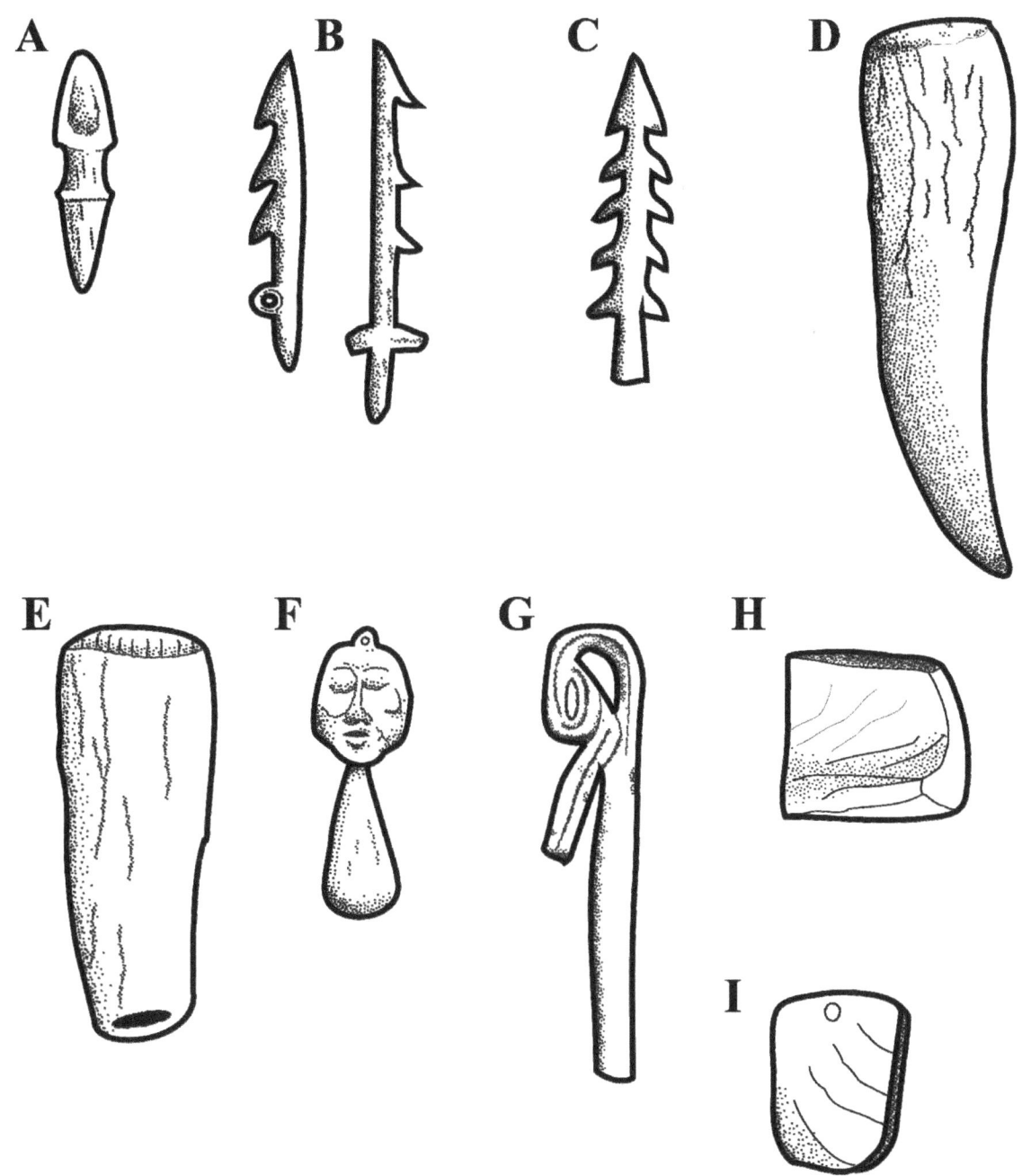

Figure 5.5 Artifacts of Antler and Shell

Antler
(A) Composite toggling harpoon valve. (B) Unilaterally barbed harpoons.
(C) Barbed point. (D) Wedge. (E) Haft. (F) Pendant. (G) Decorated or
decorative object.

Shell
(H) Edge tool. (I) Pendant/gorget.
Not to scale.

Artifacts of Antler

Composite toggling harpoon valves: part of a composite fishing tool. Two antler valves, often but not always symmetrical, held a ground stone or bone point in one end and connected to a long shaft via a foreshaft at the other end. See Figure 5.5, Item A.
Unilaterally barbed harpoons: antler points with barbs on one side. Used in fishing. See Figure 5.5, Item B.
Barbed points: fixed antler points with barbs. See Figure 5.5, Item C.
Wedges: pieces of antler that have been ground and used as a wedge. Used in splitting wood. See Figure 5.5, Item D.
Hafts: antler used as a mounting handle for another tool. These include celts, knives, etc… See Figure 5.5, Item E.
Pendants: ground antler objects used as decoration and hung by suspension. See Figure 5.5, Item F.
Decorated or decorative objects: all decorated antler objects and items for personal adornment, excluding pendants. See Figure 5.5, Item G.

Artifacts of Shell

Edge tools: all shell artifacts with a prepared edge used for cutting or scraping. These include shell knives, celts and scrapers. See Figure 5.5, Item H.
Pendant/gorgets: shell objects used for decoration or personal adornment that are not shell beads. See Figure 5.5, Item I.

The Burley (1980) typology has fifty-one more or less discrete formed artifact types. The typology does not allow for miscellaneous artifacts. Artifacts which could not be assigned to one of the fifty-one types were not included in this study. Therein lays a major criticism I have with the use of Burley's (1980) typology.

There are several important artifacts not represented in Burley's (1980) typology. The most important is the exclusion of ground slate knives. Burley (1980, 1983, Burley and Beattie 1987) argues for the importance of thin ground slate knives in Marpole assemblages as evidence for not only a subsistence base specialized on salmon but also a population replacement in the Gulf of Georgia. It would be very useful to see how changes in the distribution of ground slate knives within the Marpole culture type relate to Burley's (1980, 1983, Burley and Beattie 1987) dislocation explanation, but sadly this is not easily possible with his typology. Burley (1980) created his typology before Matson et al. (1980) study thus it is difficult to compare Burley's typology to the subphases of Marpole.

My second criticism deals with the problem of fragmentary data. By the simple nature of archaeology, most artifacts recovered are broken. Archaeology is the study of what is discarded or misplaced. Few whole artifacts are recovered unless they entered the archaeological record by accident. The majority of artifacts have been broken and discarded. In many cases these broken artifacts were too fragmentary to fit one of Burley's (1980) pigeon holes. This problem, if uniformly applied would be of less concern but Burley's (1980) typology affects these fragmentary artifacts differently. Fragmentary bone artifacts are numerous at several of the study area sites, most noticeably at Kosapsom. They are most likely broken pieces of bone unipoints, bipoints, awls, or needles. These artifacts cannot be included in this study because there is no classification for them and thus are excluded.

In contrast, virtually all fragmentary chipped stone artifacts are included in this study. Burley's (1980) category of flake edge tool encompasses all flakes, broken or not, that have been utilized or retouched in any way. This means any broken chipped stone artifact is also a flake edge tool. The artifact class is the broadest tool type in this study and as such is relatively over-represented. Another chipped stone artifact that is similarly over-represented is formed bifacial cutting and/or scraping tools. Chipped stone projectile points, which Burley (1980) divides into five types: corner-notch/basal-notch points, leaf shaped points, contracting stem points, expanding stem points and triangular points, are all also formed bifaces. In several instances where fragmentation left only a projectile point tip without the diagnostic base, I was left to classify the point as a formed biface.

These two tool types, flake edge tool and formed bifacial cutting and/or scraping tool have a degree of breadth, due to Burley's (1980) classification system, that other tool types do not. This means similarly conceived broken artifacts of bone, antler or other raw material would be excluded from the study, where their chipped stone counterparts would be included.

This problem becomes significant in the interpretation. Matson et al. (1980) notes a generalized shift away from chipped and ground stone artifacts towards bone and antler industries from Old Musqueam subphase through Beach Grove to Garrison. This use of artifact industries for interpretation is troubling given the lack of standardized treatment the Burley (1980) typology gives these different industries.

In an attempt to address this problem I have chosen to collect data on six additional artifact types, miscellaneous chipped stone, miscellaneous ground stone, miscellaneous pecked stone, miscellaneous worked bone, miscellaneous worked antler and miscellaneous worked shell. These miscellaneous categories cannot be used in conjunction with the original (Matson et al. 1980) study as this information was not collected for their original site components. I had proposed to run a separate metric multidimensional scaling test on Southern Vancouver Island sites in isolation including the miscellaneous artifact categories. This would have given some indication of the importance of the exclusion of miscellaneous artifact types from the original Matson et al. (1980) study. Unfortunately, with only seven site components the utility of such a statistic is questionable. In the absence of statistics it is sufficient to say the exclusion of miscellaneous artifact categories affects the scaling results. If interpretations are to be based on the relative proportions of tool industries then it should be noted that the complete industry is not always presented in the analysis.

The case of the miscellaneous artifact types provides an important cautionary tale to keep in mind during interpretation. The amount of miscellaneous artifacts present in site components varied greatly from as little as 5.5% at Quick's Pond to 30.75% at Kosapsom. When conclusions are made regarding the composition of artifact assemblages it must be stressed that many of the artifacts are not represented and that the process of distortion is not uniform.

Having said that, it is important to note that all the site components in this study were recorded using the same typology. The typology may over-represent flaked stone artifacts but it does not vary from site to site. Thus, it may not be perfect but at least it has been uniformly applied.

Analysis

Multidimensional scaling refers to a group of statistical procedures which compress complex data sets into what is essentially a map of variation (Hodson et al. 1966). Differences in rank order between site components are averaged to create a distance matrix. A pair-wise comparison of all site components establishes a distance measure for each site component in relation to all other sites. Figure 5.6, shows a familiar example of a distance matrix and a multidimensional scaling output. Air distances between United States cities are shown and plotted using multidimensional scaling. The multidimensional scaling output reflects the geographic relationships of the cities with distances proportional to actual air distances between the cities.

Distance matrices are transferred to two dimensional space using a measure of distance, most often city-block or Euclidean distance. City-block distance plots the distance matrix using straight lines at right angles to each

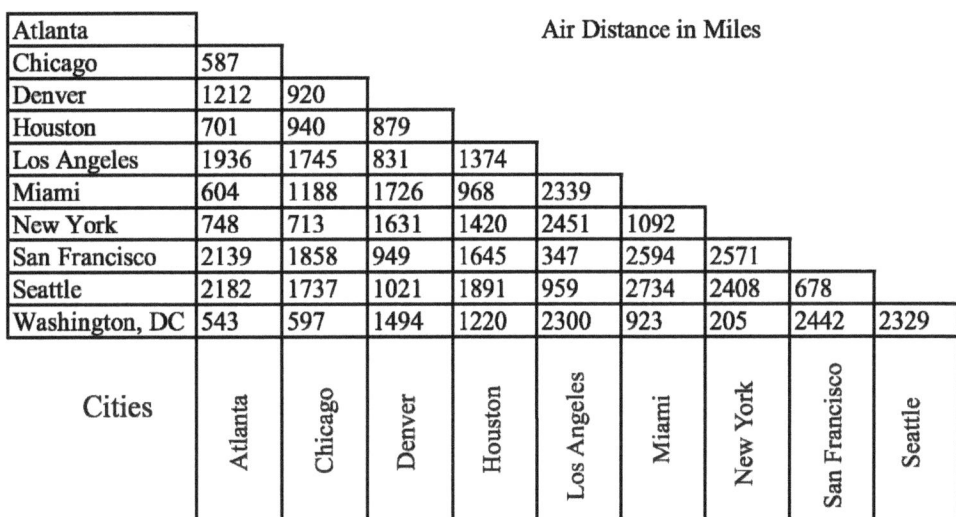

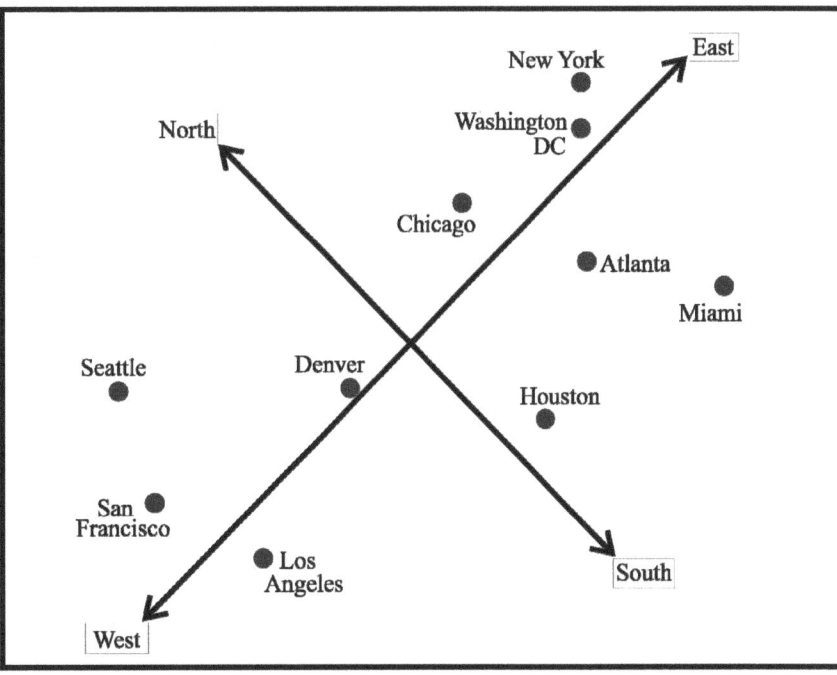

Figure 5.6 Distance Matrix and Multidimensional Scaling of Air Distance between 10 U.S. Cities.
after: Kruskal and Wish 1978:8-9.

other. Thus if point A is 5 units from point B, then city-block could plot the points any combination of movement that adds to 5, i.e. two up, three over; one down, four over etc.. The distances between all points are generated in this fashion and plotted on a diagram. In contrast, Euclidean distance refers to a straight line of distance. As city-block forms the right angle sides to a triangle, Euclidean is the hypotenuse. Figure 5.7, shows a simple diagram that explains the difference between city block and Euclidean distance. Here the distance between point A and B is 5. City block distance plots point B1 and Euclidean distance plots point B2. Note that point B is not plotted in the same place. Use of different distance measures produces different multidimensional graphs.

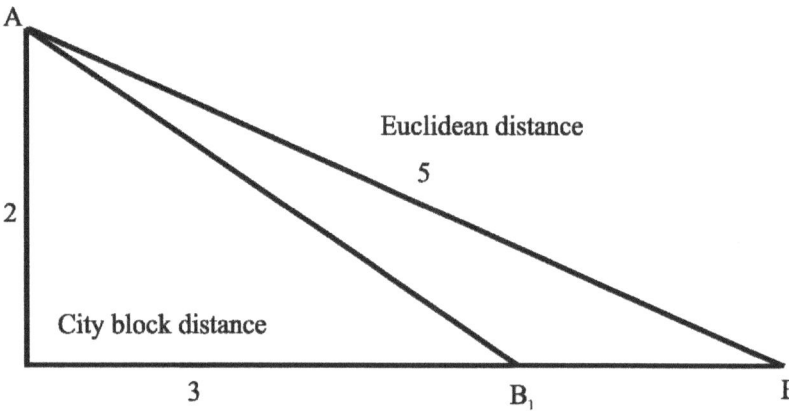

Figure 5.7 City Block versus Euclidean Distance

Non-metric multidimensional scaling was developed in Psychology to find patterns in complex non-metric data such as perceived colour or opinion (Kruskal and Wish 1978). Metric multidimensional scaling is a similar procedure developed for use with metric data.

Burley (1980) used non-metric multidimensional scaling of raw artifact frequency of eighteen Marpole components in his Ph.D. dissertation (1979), to examine variability within the Marpole culture type. Matson et al. (1980) reworked Burley's (1980) study with slightly different data and statistics. Metric multidimensional scaling based on proportional data was used in place of Burley's (1980) non-metric, raw count statistic. Burley has admitted that sample size skews his dimension one (Burley 1980). By using proportional artifact data, as with metric multidimensional scaling, each site component has equal weighting. The Burley (1980) technique gives undo "pull" to sites with large sample sizes (Matson et al. 1980). Metric multidimensional scaling is similar to the non-metric version but has some important added features. In non-metric multidimensional scaling the importance of each dimension in relation to other dimensions is unclear.

Metric multidimensional scaling places dimensions in order of importance. Thus, dimension one is the most important, i.e., accounts for the greatest variation, dimension two is the next most important and so on. The non-metric version does not rank dimensions in order of significance. This means that dimension eight may be the most significant followed by dimension three or dimension six. In this regard metric multidimensional scaling provides a more user-friendly output which allows for easier interpretation. This also eliminates the need for external criteria in determining the significance of each dimension. Also, Metric statistical procedures are better suited to data which is metric such as the archaeological data used in this thesis (Anderberg 1977, Matson et al. 1980).

The subphases of Marpole were discovered by the multidimensional scaling routines used in Matson et al. (1980). Twenty well documented site components were analyzed with metric multidimensional scaling using city-block distance. In the original Matson et al. (1980:103) study dimensions one and two accounted for 32.8% and 12.3% of variation respectively (see Figure 2.5). For my thesis I will simply replicate this study with the inclusion of the Southern Vancouver Island sites overlain onto this figure. Matson et al.'s (1980) interprets these two dimensions as representing a chronological seriation, with each cluster representing a subphase distinct in time but forming a continuum. The radiocarbon dates associated with those sites correspond roughly with that interpretation. The addition of Southern Vancouver Island sites will test the seriation explanation further.

The next two dimensions represent a further 17.8% of variance combined (Figure 2.7). Both Burley (1980) and Matson et al. (1980) agree that some of this variation is based on location, with mainland and island sites plotting separately. This mainland versus island dichotomy will also be tested by exposure to Southern Vancouver Island sites.

Multidimensional scaling allows a broad based multivariate analysis for multiple site components. In this study multidimensional scaling is ideal for the analysis of the thesis question. However, many other statistical procedures will offer similar results and may in fact be more applicable to this study (Matson, pers. comm.). Metric multidimensional scaling is chosen so that the results will be directly comparable with previous studies (Matson 1974, Matson et al. 1980, Burley 1980). This will allow Northwest Coast archaeologists without an extensive statistical background to more easily orient my study within the larger field of Northwest Coast Archaeology.

Matson et al. (1980) used cluster analysis of the scaling results for dimensions one and two to aid in their interpretation. Cluster analysis is another statistical procedure which compresses complex data into a more manageable graphic depiction (Baxter 1994). Cluster analysis groups variables together based on similarity or separates them based on difference. Using techniques like nearest neighbor or Ward's method, pairs of cases are compared to each other. After cases have been compared to each other and coefficients of similarity or difference are calculated the cases are grouped together using a clustering algorithm. In the case of an agglometrative procedure, the pair of cases with the most similarity is grouped together. In this instance the new cluster takes on the average attributes of the cases that formed the cluster. With each subsequent step another pair of cases is clustered together until the entire data set is joined. The graphical depiction shows a hierarchical dendrogram branching out to each case.

In the Matson et al. (1980) study, cluster analysis using Ward's Method produced a graphical picture of the three subphases of Marpole (see Figure 2.6). The branches of the dendrogram separated Old Musqueam, Beach Grove and Garrison components from each other.
This clustering technique will also be employed in this thesis. The level of significance of branches is often difficult to determine. Whether one chooses to separate a dendrogram into two, three, or ten branches is a arbitrary assignment. This decision must be based on external variables as there is no inherent significance in each branch. Thus, Matson et al. (1980) may have chosen to interpret the presence of two clusters or six, however they chose three clusters based on the results of multidimensional scaling. Since it is difficult to assess the significance of cluster analysis, it is used primarily as an interpretive tool for the multidimensional scaling results.

Southern Vancouver Island
Artifact data from seven Southern Vancouver Island sites has be added to existing data from twenty Gulf of Georgia sites (Matson et al. 1980). Using Tscale, a metric multidimensional scaling program developed by R.G. Matson (n.d.) I have replicated the Matson et al. (1980) study with the addition of Southern Vancouver Island data. Ward's Cluster Analysis using SPSS 7.5 has been performed on the scaling results from dimensions one and two.

The results of multidimensional scaling and cluster analysis are being compared to the three working hypotheses, outlined in Chapter Four, for interpretation in the following chapter. These working hypotheses provide possible explanations for this study. It is also possible that there is an explanation not presented in the working hypotheses that may be discovered in analysis.
The first working hypothesis is that the Old Musqueam subphase of Marpole begins in the Fraser River and slowly diffuses to the islands (Matson and Coupland 1995). If this hypothesis is proven then the data from Southern Vancouver Island should overlap with the Beach Grove and Garrison subphases and not the Old Musqueam subphase.

The second working hypothesis is based on classification error. In this scenario, assemblages thought to be Locarno Beach culture type may in fact be the Old Musqueam subphase of Marpole assemblages. Support for this hypothesis would be the grouping of some Southern Vancouver Island with other Old Musqueam subphase components from the rest of the Gulf of Georgia region.

The third working hypothesis sees an absence of Marpole on Southern Vancouver Island. If this hypothesis is supported then all Southern Vancouver Island should group separately and not overlap the Matson et al. (1980) site clusters. Whereas Matson et al. (1980) grouped their sites into three subphases the Southern Vancouver Island should then cluster in one or two groups removed from the other Gulf of Georgia sites.

The results from both multidimensional scaling studies will then be compared to radiocarbon dates obtained for the sites. Many of the study area sites have radiocarbon dates which will be used to help interpret the multidimensional scaling results. Radiocarbon dating will help correlate the data patterns discovered with regard to the accepted regional sequence.

This chapter discussed the data collection and quality as well as the extensive reclassification scheme undertaken. It described the coding, multidimensional scaling, and clustering procedures that will be employed in this thesis. This chapter has related the means by which the thesis question will be tested against the data and how radiocarbon data will be used to clarify the findings. The next chapter will interpret the results of this study and attempt to integrate the findings into the greater field of Northwest Coast Archaeology.

CHAPTER 6. RESULTS

This chapter provides a description of the results of the metric multidimensional scaling analysis specified in the previous chapter. Chapter Seven presents an interpretation of the patterns described here and relates to the previously described working hypotheses and explanations of culture change. This chapter shows results for the first four dimensions of variation of multidimensional scaling and Ward's cluster analysis and relates these findings to previous studies.

The metric multidimensional output of dimensions one and two, shown in Figure 6.1, shows the separation of four clusters. Note that site component abbreviations are given in Tables 2.5 and 5.1. Dimensions one and two account for 33.49% and 10.59% of total variation respectively (see Appendix Four). The first three clusters uphold the pattern, albeit inverted, as described by Matson et al. (1980) in their study. (see Chapter Two, Figure 2.5) These clusters represent the Garrison, Beach Grove and Old Musqueam subphases. The fourth cluster is a new creation which contains only Southern Vancouver Island sites, which I have labeled Bowker Creek, following the tradition of naming archaeological cultures after the first well described single component site from which the culture was discovered (see Matson et al. 1980:113). Bowker Creek was chosen because all other sites save for Northwest Cadboro Bay are multicomponent. Northwest Cadboro Bay could be easily confused with Cadboro Bay which is a larger and generally better known site. Bowker Creek remains the first well documented single component site (Mitchell (1979) and thus, will be used to name this cluster.

Cluster one, which Matson et al. (1980) label the Garrison subphase remains as described by them. The components of this cluster are: Deep Bay II, Point Grey, Garrison, English Bluff, False Narrows I, False Narrows II, Montague Harbour II and Beach Grove 57, 61, and 79. There are no newly added Southern Vancouver Island sites in this cluster. These sites have a wide geographic spread from Garrison in the south to Deep Bay II in the north, with many of the sites located in the Gulf Islands. See Figure 6.2, for a map of site distribution.

The Garrison subphase dates to the later half of the Marpole culture type (Matson et al. 1980, Matson and Coupland 1995). Matson et al. (1980) interpret Garrison as the most recent of the subphases although there is some ambiguity in radiocarbon dating.

Garrison components are dominated by artifacts made of bone. The bone industry comprises 31.65% of the site assemblages, by far the highest contribution of bone to any of the subphases in this study. Antler and pecked stone also make contributions which are higher than all other subphases. Table 6.1, shows a summary of each subphase and the relative proportion of each artifact industry.

Cluster Two, Beach Grove, also remains as described in Matson et al. (1980). This cluster consists of: Helen Point IIA, Helen Point IIB, Hill Site, Whalen Farm, Marpole II, Beach Grove 80 and Beach Grove 62. There are no newly added Southern Vancouver Island sites in this cluster. The site components of this cluster come from the Lower Mainland and the Gulf Islands. See Figure 6.2, for a map of site distribution.

Matson et al. (1980) place the Beach Grove subphase between Garrison and Old Musqueam in the regional culture sequence. As with the Garrison subphase there is ambiguity with the radiocarbon dating of this subphase, however there is a strong formal argument for Beach Grove predating Garrison. The artifact assemblages of Beach Grove appear transitionary between Garrison and Old Musqueam. When compared to Garrison, Beach Grove has relatively more chipped stone and less bone and pecked stone artifacts. This pattern of decreased importance of chipped stone has been noted as a general trend which takes place from Locarno Beach through Marpole to Gulf of Georgia (Matson and Coupland 1995, Mitchell 1990). The trend is also echoed within the Marpole culture type with a decrease from Old Musqueam through Beach Grove to Garrison (Matson et al. 1980, Matson and Coupland 1995).

Typically diagnostic artifacts associated with Locarno Beach and early Marpole, such as composite toggling harpoon valves, microblades and labrets, are all found in decreasing frequency beginning in Old Musqueam with fewer still in Beach Grove and are entirely absent from the Garrison subphase. Artifacts associated with the Gulf of Georgia culture type such as small triangular ground stone projectile points, unilaterally barbed harpoons and hand mauls are found in higher frequencies in Garrison, and lower frequencies in Beach Grove and are all but absent in Old Musqueam.

The third cluster, named Old Musqueam by Matson et al. (1980) changes from the initial study. Two Southern Vancouver Island sites, Quick's Pond and DcRu 572 are additions to this cluster. As before, the other site components are: Old Musqueam, Glenrose Cannery III, Crescent Beach III, Fossil Bay I, and Musqueam Northeast. Matson and Coupland (1995) have argued for a Fraser River Delta "birthplace" for the Marpole culture as all but one of the Old Musqueam subphase components were located on the Lower Mainland. This interpretation appears to be a product of their limited sample rather than a valid result. This thesis adds two

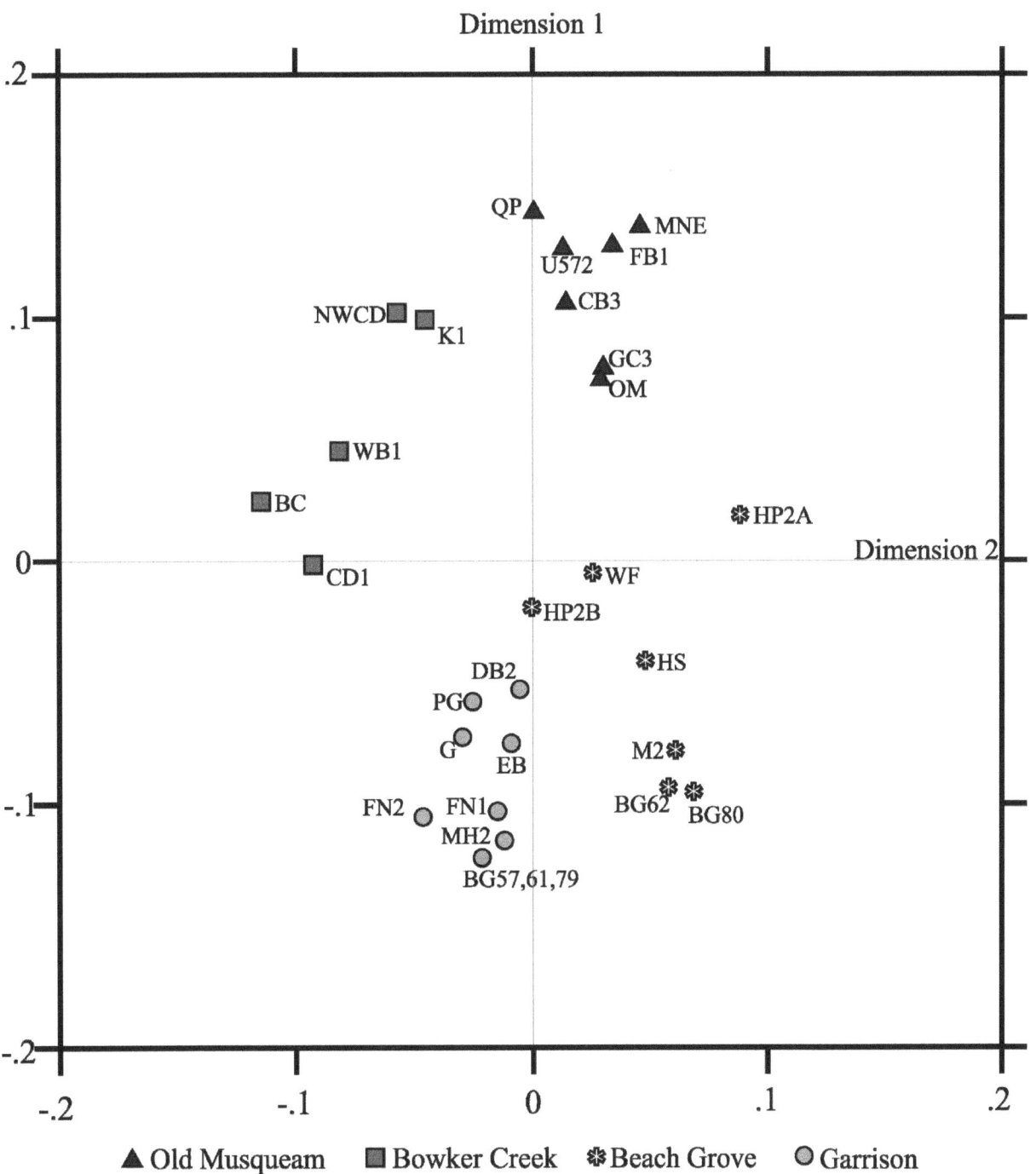

Figure 6.1 Metric Multidimensional Scaling for 27 Gulf of Georgia Marpole Components Using City Block Distance. Dimensions 1 and 2.

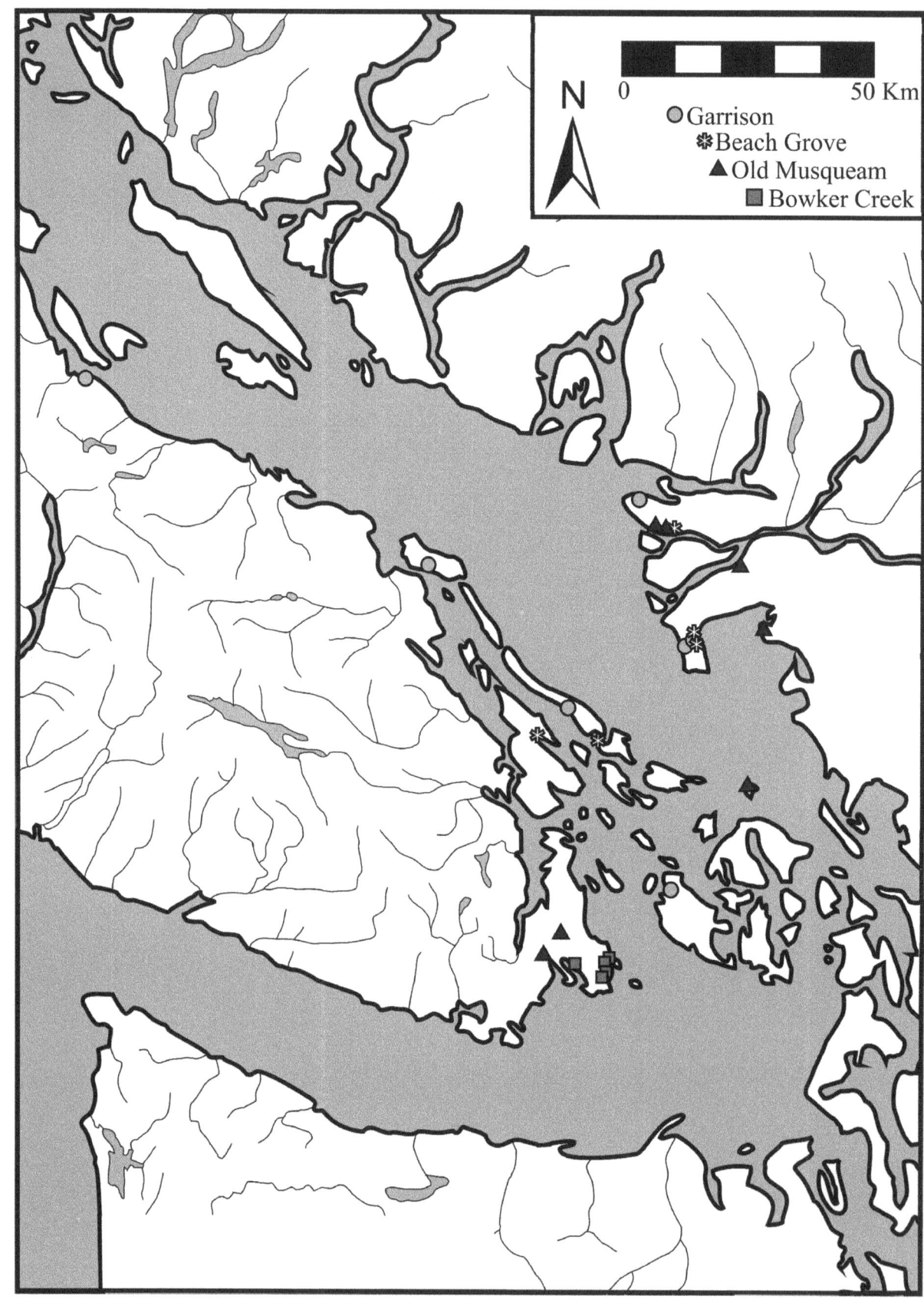

Figure 6.2 Map of Gulf of Georgia, Locarno Beach and Marpole Subphase Components

	Garrison		Beach Grove		Old Musqueam		Bowker Creek	
	Mean	Range	Mean	Range	Mean	Range	Mean	Range
Total chipped stone	21.3%	8.8-32.0%	31.6%	16.2-43.9%	65.7%	54.3-77.9%	56.0%	43.7-66.3%
total ground stone	23.2%	15.3-32.9%	38.8%	23.2-47.5%	18.1%	11.1-28.3%	17.8%	13.7-22.7%
total pecked stone	6.5%	0-18.0%	3.7%	0.8-7.4%	4.7%	1.8-12.7%	2.9%	1.7-4.4%
total bone	31.7%	27.8-34.7%	16.4%	4.3-29.4%	8.7%	0.5-21.7%	13.3%	6.1-21.0%
total antler	14.6%	9.5-16.5%	8.8%	2.2-17.4%	2.4%	0.0-4.4%	5.8%	2.0-12.2%
total shell	2.8%	0.0-9.1%	0.7%	0.0-3.9%	0.5%	0.0-1.8%	4.2%	1.9-9.8%
sample size	152.8	70-330	147.4	68-288	158.0	56-258	317.4	101-758
number of sites	8		7		7		5	

Table 6.1 Cluster Composition by Artifact Industry

new site components to this subphase and the dates are equally as old as the Old Musqueam subphase components from the Fraser River Delta. See Figure 6.2, for a map of site distribution. My results thus call into question the origin of the Marpole culture type, as will be discussed further in the next chapter.

The assemblage composition for Old Musqueam remains much like the original Matson et al. (1980) study. Chipped stone predominates the assemblage accounting for 65.68% of the total. Bone, antler and shell continue to provide little to the total artifact frequency (see Table 6.1. Matson et al. (1980) noted that hand mauls were limited to the later Beach Grove and Garrison subphases and that none were found in association with Old Musqueam deposits. Quick's Pond, which has been added to the Old Musqueam subphase has one hand maul in its assemblage. However, this site is a surface collected lithic scatter which possesses traits of both Locarno Beach and Marpole, it is possible that there has been some mixing within what may be a multicomponent site.

The fourth cluster contains exclusively Southern Vancouver Island sites. The site components are: Willows Beach I, Kosapsom I, Cadboro Bay I, Northwest Cadboro Bay, and Bowker Creek.

The Bowker Creek cluster is most closely related to Old Musqueam with its high percentage of chipped stone 56.04% (see Table 6.1). It differs with a much higher proportion of bone artifacts, 13.32% as compared to 8.67% in Old Musqueam. Bowker Creek possesses the highest percentage of shell artifacts in this study 4.15%, almost all of which are shell edge tools.

Figure 6.3, shows Ward's Cluster Analysis of dimensions one and two of the metric multidimensional scaling results. This figure shows the clear separation of each cluster and the close association of Garrison and Beach Grove, and Old Musqueam and Bowker Creek. The internal organization of the Garrison and Beach Grove clusters varies somewhat from the initial Matson et al. (1980) (reproduced in Chapter Two, Figure 2.6) study but the pattern remains strong.

The interpretation of dimension one given by Burley (1980) and Matson et al. (1980) relates to the proportion of stone to bone artifacts in the component assemblages. Components with a large ratio of stone artifacts to bone appear in the top of dimension one. In contrast, those site

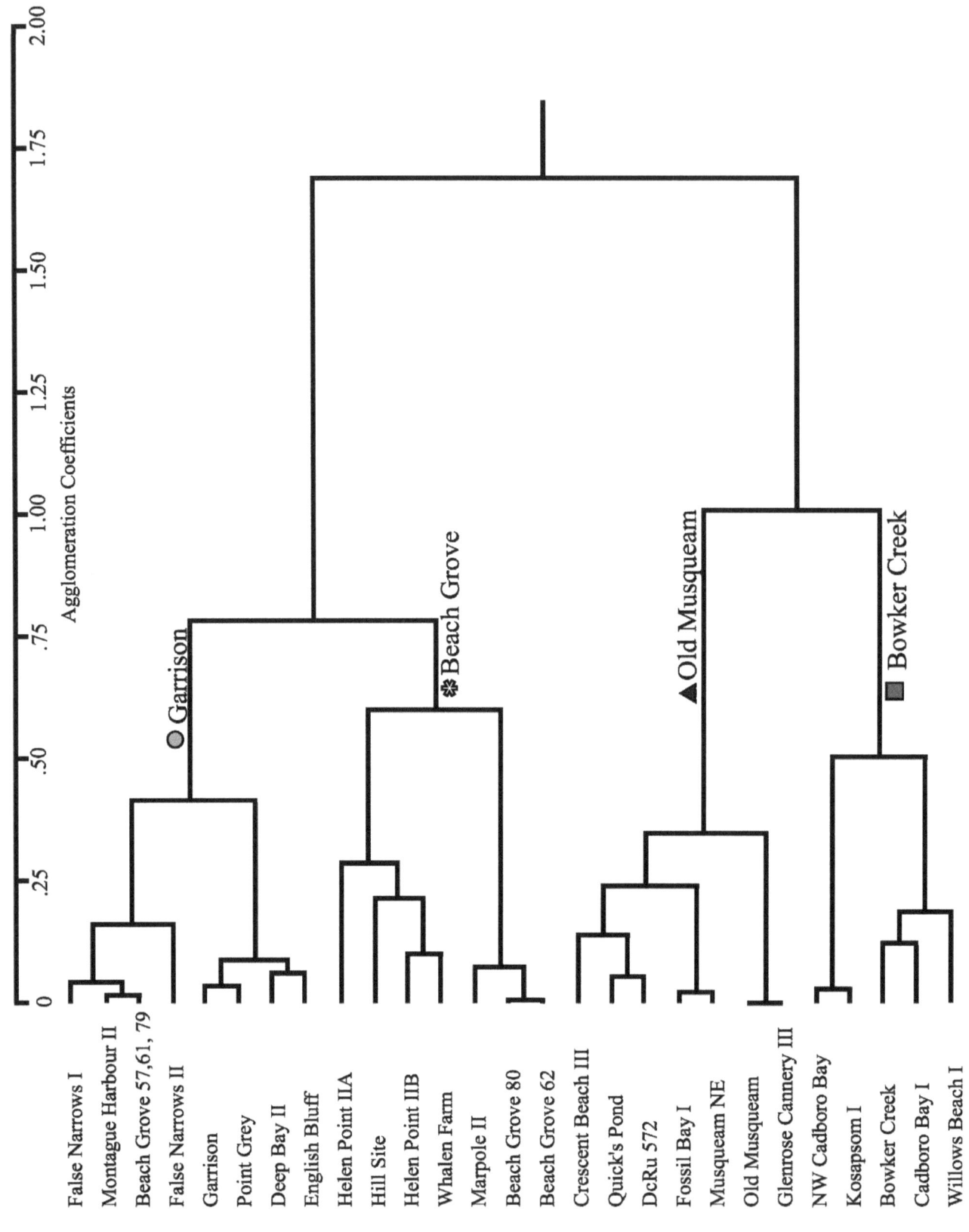

Figure 6.3 Ward's Cluster Analysis of Dimensions 1 and 2 of Metric Multidimensional Scaling Results.

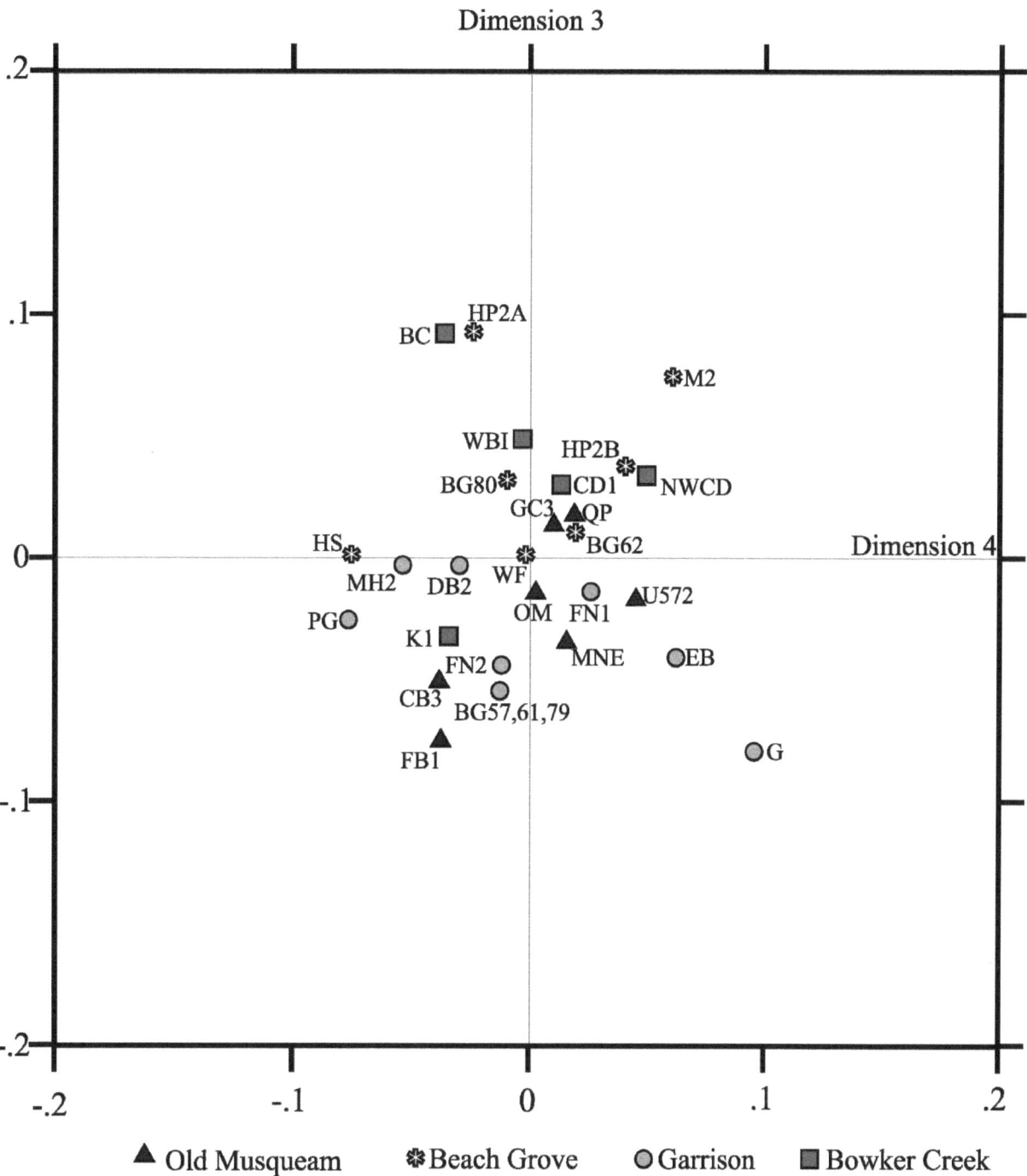

Figure 6.4 Metric Multidimensional Scaling Results for 27 Gulf of Georgia Marpole Components Using City Block Distance.

components with low stone artifact to bone artifact ratios appear on the bottom of dimension one. In Figure 6.1, this can seen with the Old Musqueam and Bowker Creek clusters near the top and the Beach Grove and Garrison clusters near the bottom of dimension one. This pattern continues in this study and I share Burley (1980 and Matson's (Matson et al. 1980) interpretation of dimension one.

According to Burley (1980), dimension two may either represent time or site function. Matson et al. (1980) specify this interpretation by noting that the arc pattern of Clusters one, two and three are most likely a linear chronological procession bent into a horseshoe by the nature of the statistical procedure. Dimension two is then interpreted as representing time, but not, in a direct straight line but rather as points on a curved arc. In this study that pattern continues. Aside from being inverted, the relationship of the Old Musqueam, Beach Grove and Garrison clusters remains intact. These clusters form a horseshoe with the oldest site components near the top and the youngest ones near the bottom. The new cluster, Bowker Creek attaches to the Old Musqueam end of the horseshoe. Following this interpretation, Bowker Creek should then be the oldest of the clusters, which is partially true. The oldest components in this study date to the Bowker Creek cluster. There is however, a large temporal range for Bowker Creek. Radiocarbon dates for the Bowker Creek cluster span much of the range of Marpole. The variation expressed as the Bowker Creek cluster cannot be simply interpreted as temporal. There are other factors which must explain the separation of a new and distinct cluster which does not fit into the accepted regional sequence. This interpretation will be given in the next chapter. As well, the meaning of all four clusters and the relationships between them will be discussed.

Dimensions three and four are represented in Figure 6.4. These two dimensions account for 8.79% and 7.33% of the total variation. Burley (1980) and Matson et al. (1980) interpreted dimensions three and four as Mainland versus Gulf Island assemblages (see Figure 2.7). In this study there has been considerable reshuffling of dimensions three and four. At present I do not have an interpretation of the pattern seen in Figure 6.4, although it is clear that the Mainland versus Gulf Islands distinction is no longer evident.

This chapter described the results of metric multidimensional scaling and cluster analysis. The next chapter will explain the meaning of these results in relation to the working hypotheses and the explanations of culture change that were presented in previous chapters.

CHAPTER 7. INTERPRETATION OF RESULTS

This chapter will present my interpretations of the patterns discovered in this thesis. This interpretation will take three forms. The first will be a re-examination of the regional culture historical sequence with the inclusion of the new data presented in this thesis. The second will be a revisitation of the working hypotheses described in Chapter Four. In this section I will choose which hypothesis, if any, best suits the patterns discovered. Lastly, the explanations of culture change will be reexamined. These explanations will be compared against my results to see if any can possibly be supported by the data. Arising from this discussion, I will offer my own view of culture change across the Locarno Beach - Marpole transition.

The currently accepted regional sequence, as shown in Figure 7.1, shows a progression from the Locarno Beach culture type to the Marpole culture type at 2500/2400 BP and then to the Gulf of Georgia culture type by 1500/1100 BP. Marpole is further subdivided into three subphases of roughly equal length which are chronologically linked: Old Musqueam, Beach Grove, and Garrison, oldest to youngest (see Chapter Two for a more detailed discussion). My results, (see Chapter Six), show the continuation of these subphases and the addition of a fourth one named Bowker Creek.

sequence. As shown in Figure 6.1, the multidimensional scaling results show an association between the Bowker Creek and Old Musqueam subphases. This pattern is better illustrated in Figure 6.3, where cluster analysis clearly links Bowker Creek with Old Musqueam, and separates it from the Beach Grove and Garrison subphases.

There seem to be two possible explanations for this pattern. First, following the interpretation of Matson et al. (1980), who describe Old Musqueam as representative of early Marpole and Beach Grove and Garrison as variants of late Marpole, Bowker Creek with its close ties to Old Musqueam may be thought of as another variant of early Marpole. In this instance, the sites of Bowker Creek, Willows Beach, Quick's Pond and others originally identified as Locarno Beach would rather be representative of early Marpole. This would also serve to push back the initial date of Marpole from 2500/2400 BP to closer to 3000 BP.

The second possibility is that Old Musqueam and Bowker Creek are not related to the Marpole culture type at all. The large separation seen in Figure 6.3, may be indicative of a more dramatic shift in the regional culture historical sequence than simply the shift from early Marpole to late Marpole. In this case Old Musqueam and Bowker Creek may be more appropriately assigned to the Locarno Beach culture type and the cluster separation shown in Figure 6.3 denotes the Locarno Beach - Marpole transition. In this case the date of the Locarno Beach to Marpole transition moves forward to 2000 BP in the Fraser River delta and Gulf Islands, while Southern Vancouver Island would lack Marpole altogether.

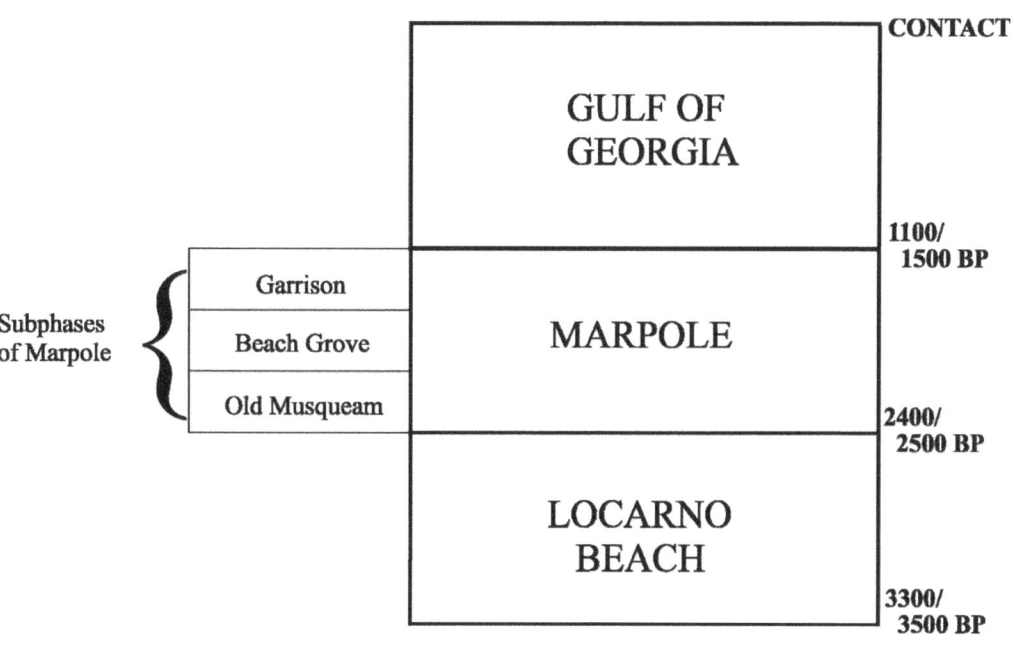

Figure 7.1 Currently Accepted Regional Culture History for the Gulf of Georgia

The position of the new Bowker Creek subphase in relation to the other subphases is central to my reinterpretation of the regional culture historical

I will now examine both these positions based on formal, temporal and spatial criteria. Artifactual assemblage composition was the sole attribute measured in the metric multidimensional scaling and clustering procedures employed in this thesis. The four subphase clusters were identified base on formal groupings and as such formal criteria are the strongest line of evidence. Temporal and geographic data are used to support the line of formal reasoning and aid in its interpretation.

My analysis of the formal evidence will begin with a look at artifact industries and then switch to a focus on individual artifact types thought to be indicative of the Locarno Beach - Marpole transition. Although I have been critical of the comparison of artifact industries in interpretation (see Chapter Five), the exercise is still worthwhile. Accepting the inherent flaws of the Burley (1980) typology which unduly weights some industries over others the comparison does treat subphases equally.

The average proportion of artifact industry is shown in Table 6.1. Chipped stone is far greater in Old Musqueam and Bowker Creek assemblages, 65.68% and 56.04% as compared to 31.64% and 21.32% for Beach Grove and Garrison, respectively. Inversely, ground stone, bone and antler all make significantly stronger contributions to Beach Grove and Garrison than to Old Musqueam and Bowker Creek. These industry comparisons seem to show a clear separation of Beach Grove and Garrison from Old Musqueam and Bowker Creek.

This pattern will be further explored by examining a few key artifact types which have been thought of as diagnostic traits for Locarno Beach and/or Marpole; labrets, hand mauls, and microblades will serve as examples.

First, labrets are listed as a diagnostic trait for both the Locarno Beach and Marpole culture type. (see Tables 2.1 and 2.3). Taking a closer look at their distribution, it seems that labrets are widespread in Locarno Beach and occur only in the Old Musqueam subphase of Marpole. There is only one exception to this rule, that being the Hill Site on Saltspring Island (Hall and Haggarty 1981). However, Matson and Coupland (1995) have questioned the association of labrets to the Beach Grove assemblage at that site. Thus labrets do not co-vary between Locarno Beach and Marpole if Old Musqueam is thought as a constituent of Locarno Beach.

The second illustrative artifact type I will discuss is hand mauls. Hand mauls are a diagnostic artifact type associated with the Marpole culture type (Mitchell 1971b, see Table 2.3). They do not appear in Locarno Beach assemblages. Matson and Coupland (1995) have argued that the distribution of hand mauls links Old Musqueam to Locarno Beach and separates it from Beach Grove and Garrison. They noted that no hand mauls were found in any of the Old Musqueam assemblages although they were relatively common in Beach Grove and Garrison sites. This thesis has assigned a single hand maul from Quick's Pond to the Old Musqueam subphase. The nature of the Quick's Pond site, a surface lithic scatter does not lend complete confidence to this assignment. It is possible that the Quick's Pond assemblage is mixed as no stratigraphy is available for this surface collected site.

The Bowker Creek cluster has two sites with hand mauls present. In both of these sites the hand mauls date to later deposits contemporaneous with Beach Grove and Garrison subphases. Thus the argument that hand mauls are only associated with post 2000 BP deposits is not substantially challenged.

The last artifactual example is that of microblades. Microblade technology is listed as a diagnostic trait for both Locarno Beach and Marpole culture types (see Tables 2.1 and 2.3). The archaeological record shows a noticeable decline in microblade abundance in Marpole as compared to Locarno Beach. The Old Musqueam and Bowker Creek clusters have considerably more microblades (2.77% and 10.57% respectively) than do Beach Grove and Garrison clusters (1.38% and 0.78% respectively). Thus microblades reiterate the differences between the two clusters.

The artifact assemblages demonstrate a strong separation of Old Musqueam and Bowker Creek from Beach Grove and Garrison. The three examples show that key diagnostic artifacts types do not co-vary between the two large clusters. This pattern is echoed by other artifact types, most notably pièces esquillées, several chipped and ground stone projectile points, irregular abrasive stones, decorated bone and antler, and antler wedges.

Lastly, the metric multidimensional scaling and clustering has shown that, based on formal attributes, Old Musqueam and Bowker Creek are sufficiently different from Beach Grove and Garrison to warrant their removal from the Marpole culture type.

Radiocarbon dating further strengthens the formal argument. Although I have questioned the precision of the technique relating to the Locarno Beach - Marpole transition (see Appendix One) on a general level radiocarbon dating remains a valuable interpretive tool. Figure 7.2 shows a graphical depiction of several radiocarbon age estimates for site components examined in this thesis. This, however, is not a comprehensive list. These dates are directly related to deposits of the original site components defined by Matson et al. (1980). Numerous re-excavations have occurred at these sites but as with the artifactual data, the radiocarbon data has not been updated in this thesis.

Age estimates are shown with plus or minus one standard deviation about the mean (see Appendix One). Keep in mind that the actual age of each radiocarbon sample may fall outside the range given in Figure 7.2.

The graph shows that the chronological linking of Old Musqueam, Beach Grove and Garrison remains intact. The Beach Grove and Garrison subphases roughly post-date 2100 BP and continue until the onset of the Gulf of Georgia culture type at 1500/1100 BP. Recall that Matson et al. (1980) had noted radiocarbon dating offered little help in differentiating the later subphases of Beach Grove and Garrison but there was a formal argument to do so. However there was good temporal separation between the earlier Old Musqueam and the later subphases. Radiocarbon age estimates for Old Musqueam show a range of roughly 2400 - 2000 BP.

Bowker Creek shows a large temporal range dating from well before the accepted Locarno Beach - Marpole transition with a date over 2700 BP and continuing until almost 1750 BP. There is considerable overlap between the Bowker Creek subphase and all three other subphases. With the case of Old Musqueam this does not pose a problem as both represent similar and closely related assemblages. However, overlap with later subphases does not fit with the currently accepted regional sequence, Figure 7.1. In this instance there is now a considerable overlap of earlier and later subphases for almost 350 years. The chronological development of early Marpole to late Marpole as proposed by Matson et al. (1980) can no longer be accepted. Thus the currently accepted regional culture history, Figure 7.1, no longer reflects radiocarbon data.

I will now turn to the geographic distribution of site components to further examine the validity of a new regional culture historical sequence (see map, Figure 6.2). Old Musqueam site components can be seen across the Gulf of Georgia region from the mouth of the Fraser River to the Saanich Peninsula. Beach Grove and Garrison site components occur in the Fraser Delta and the Gulf Islands. They are noticeably absent from Southern Vancouver Island. Bowker Creek components are limited to Southern Vancouver Island only. They do not occur in the Gulf Islands or on the mainland. Thus when temporal and spatial data are combined it can be seen that prior to cluster two, the Beach Grove and Garrison subphases, the Gulf of Georgia region is more or less homogeneous. Cluster one site components, represented by the Old Musqueam and Bowker Creek subphases, occur across the region with some overlap on Southern Vancouver Island. Although Bowker Creek is limited to Southern Vancouver Island its closely related counterpart, Old Musqueam exists elsewhere.

With the onset of cluster two the regional picture changes dramatically. The Fraser River Delta and Gulf Islands show Beach Grove and Garrison assemblages while Southern Vancouver Island has the Bowker Creek subphase. There is no longer a region-wide artifact assemblage. The region has bifurcated into two separate and distinct culture histories. Figures 6.1 and 6.3, show that this separation is a dramatic one. This predicament cannot be explained using the current regional culture historical sequence, Figure 7.1. Thus formal, temporal and spatial lines of the new evidence presented in this thesis support the development of a new regional culture historical sequence.

Recall that both the terms phase and culture type rely on a list of similar traits which encompass a group of assemblages and separates it from other similarly conceived groups of assemblages (see Chapter Two). Old Musqueam and Bowker Creek subphases do not share sufficient traits with Beach Grove and Garrison to be considered subphases of a single culture type. Rather, they closely mirror Locarno Beach culture type assemblages.

At this time I will propose a new a culture historical sequence, Figure 7.3, for the Gulf of Georgia. This regional sequence shows a bifurcation in the region and shows separate cultural histories for the Fraser Delta and Gulf Islands and for Southern Vancouver Island. The Marpole culture type has been reworked to include only the Beach Grove and Garrison subphases. Thus, the newly proposed temporal extent of Marpole becomes 2000 BP to 1500/1100 BP. I have reassigned the Old Musqueam subphase and added the Bowker Creek subphase to Locarno Beach. The temporal extent of Locarno Beach in the Fraser Delta and Gulf Islands is between 3500/3300 BP and 2000 BP. On Southern Vancouver Island, Locarno Beach lasts until the onset of the Gulf of Georgia culture type at 1500/1100 BP.

I feel this newly proposed regional sequence more accurately depicts the culture history of Southern Vancouver Island within the Gulf of Georgia. Several researchers (Mitchell, pers. comm., Keddie pers. comm.) have felt that Marpole was not represented on Southern Vancouver Island. The regional culture history masked the variation seen on Southern Vancouver Island and focused solely on the Fraser River and Gulf Islands for a regional interpretation. This research has shown that Southern Vancouver Island does not fit Fraser River-based depiction of culture history and a new culture history is required.

The Working Hypotheses
The working hypotheses were some of my predicted outcomes. I felt the results of this study would agree with one of them. It is now time to examine the applicability

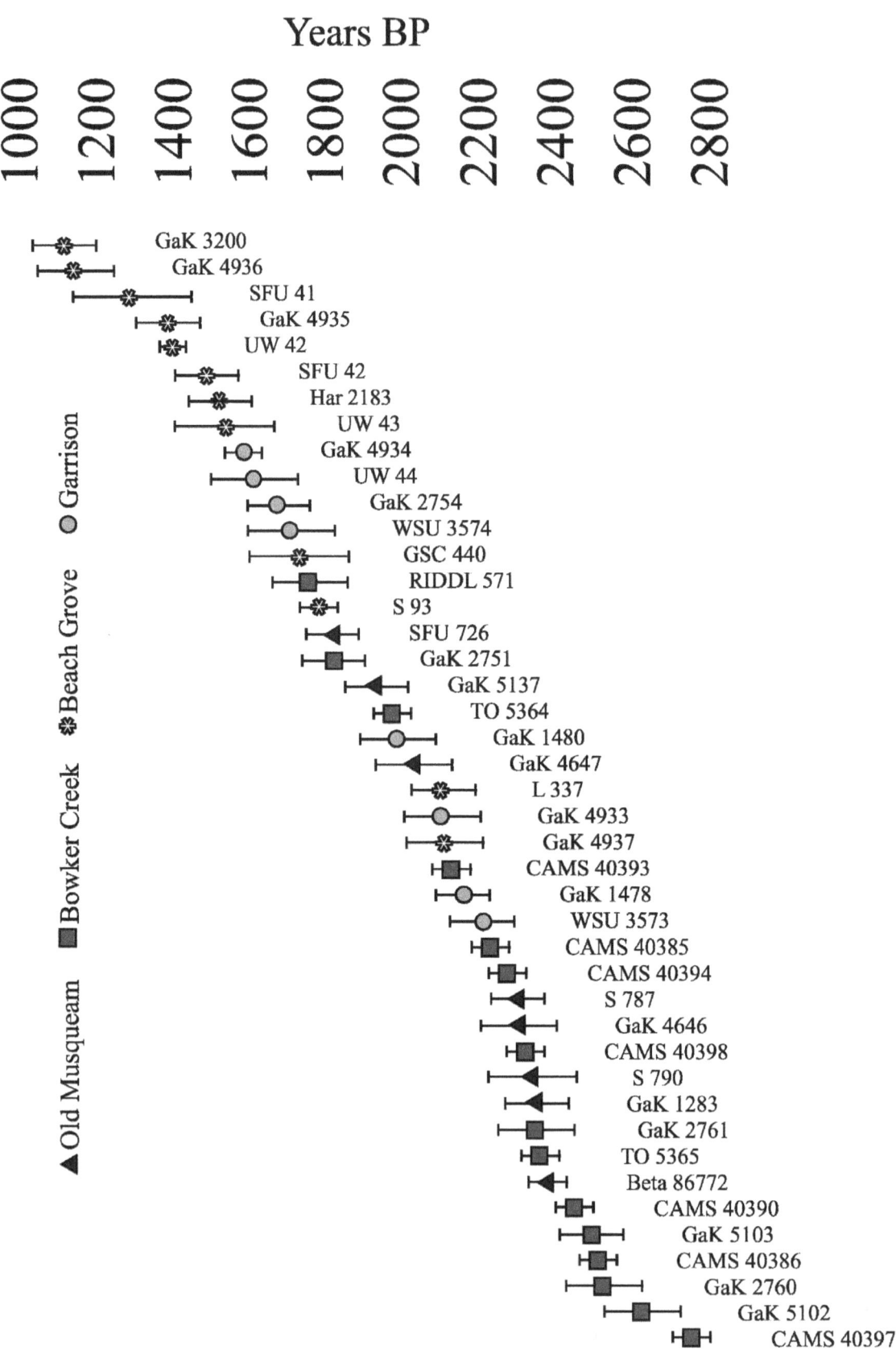

Figure 7.2 Raw Radiocarbon Age Estimates for Selected Gulf of Georgia Area Site Components.

notes: range shown equals ± one standard deviation.
dates on marine shell have been corrected -390 ± 23 BP

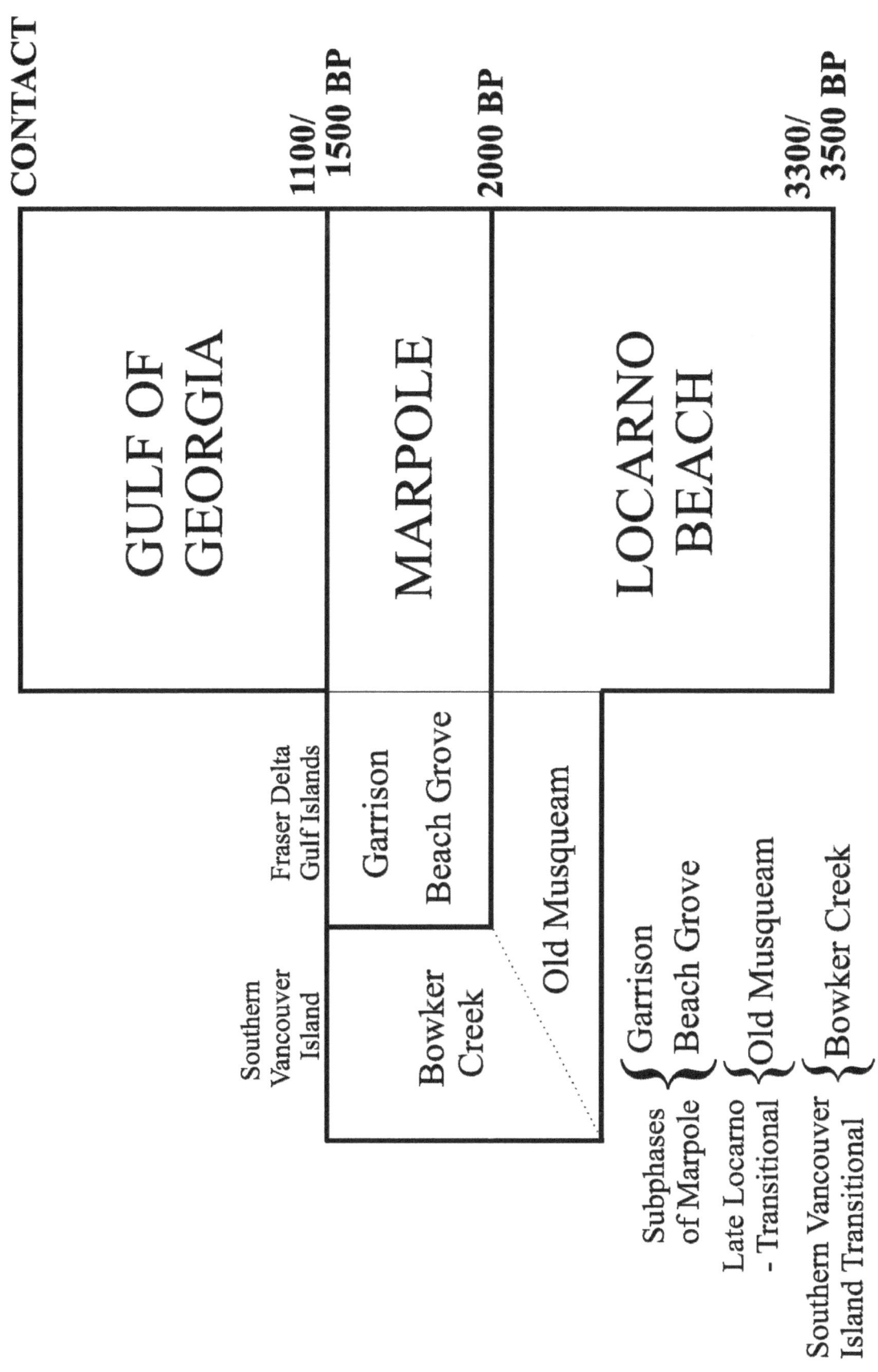

Figure 7.3 Newly Proposed Regional Culture History for the Gulf of Georgia

of those hypotheses. The first working hypothesis states that the origin of Marpole occurred at the mouth of the Fraser River. Thus, Old Musqueam should be limited to the Fraser River Delta and the subsequent Beach Grove and Garrison should spread out over the entire Gulf of Georgia region. If this hypothesis was correct then Southern Vancouver Island should show evidence of Beach Grove and Garrison but not Old Musqueam.

The data soundly reject this hypothesis. There is Old Musqueam on Southern Vancouver Island at two sites Quick's Pond and DcRu 572. In addition there are no components attributed to Beach Grove or Garrison on Southern Vancouver Island. Therefore the notion that Old Musqueam originates at the Fraser River delta and expands across the region is rejected. In fact, Southern Vancouver Island Old Musqueam components have older radiocarbon dates than do their Fraser River counterparts. This raises the question of a possible Southern Vancouver Island "birthplace" of Old Musqueam and a later diffusion to the Mainland, not vice versa. Earlier concepts of the development and spread of Marpole were a product of an unrepresentative sample; now that site data from Southern Vancouver Island have been examined this conventional view can no longer can be accepted.

The second hypothesis was that classification errors in Southern Vancouver Island assemblages had occurred. It was thought possible that some of the Southern Vancouver Island components interpreted as Locarno Beach but having Marpole dates were actually attributable to Old Musqueam but misclassified. If this hypothesis is correct then the results should show several Southern Vancouver Island sites clustering with the Old Musqueam subphase. This hypothesis is partially supported by the data. Two Southern Vancouver Island site components, Quick's Pond and DcRu 572, have been added to the Old Musqueam subphase.

However, this hypothesis was created with the thought that the sites I originally focused on, Kosapsom and Willows Beach may in fact be Old Musqueam. These sites do not cluster within the Old Musqueam subphase. Also, underlying this hypothesis was the notion that if Old Musqueam was present then so should be the later subphases. If this hypothesis was correct then all three subphases should be present and clearly they are not.

One of the predicted outcomes of the hypothesis was that the Old Musqueam subphase would be reconsidered, allowing for equally old components on Southern Vancouver Island. This aspect must now be accepted. The Old Musqueam subphase components on Southern Vancouver Island are actually older that those on the Fraser River. The temporal and spatial range of the Old Musqueam subphase has been significantly redefined by this thesis and as such Old Musqueam now requires reinterpretation.

The third working hypothesis sees an absence of Marpole altogether on Southern Vancouver Island. If supported then all three original subphases should not be present on Southern Vancouver Island. At the outset this hypothesis seems to be negated by the data as two Southern Vancouver Island sites cluster with the Old Musqueam subphase. However, since I have chosen to rework the regional sequence and consider Old Musqueam as more appropriately a subphase of Locarno Beach (see Figure 7.3), this hypothesis can also accepted. The newly defined Marpole is not known to occur in the study area. Marpole, now a culture type consisting of two subphases, Beach Grove and Garrison and lasting from 2000-1500/1100 BP is lacking from Southern Vancouver Island. Locarno Beach, expressed as Old Musqueam and Bowker Creek is present. Thus, one major conclusion of this thesis is that the Marpole culture type is not known from Southern Vancouver Island.

Explanations of Culture Change
I would now like to revisit the explanations of prehistoric culture change presented in Chapter Three. The explanations are attempts by archaeologists at describing the Locarno Beach - Marpole transition. This thesis has provided some important new information which requires the reanalysis of these explanations.

The explanations were separated into two basic theoretical positions, dislocation versus continuity (see Chapter Three). Of the dislocation explanations only Burley (1980, 1983, Burley and Beattie 1987) has offered a current and scientific explanation. Burley favours a canyon-to-coast migration in consort with a complex of interrelated processes that link salmon preservation to a host of Northwest Coast ethnographic traits such as cooperative housing, semi-sedentism, surplus production and specialization (see Figure 3.1).

The suite of processes that Burley (1980, 1983) argues feeds back and creates Marpole has not been tested in this thesis. These processes are theoretical and are conceived of and evaluated intuitively. Most of these processes are also used by continuity theorists in their attempt to explain the development of Marpole. Matson (1989) discusses how some of the aspects of the processes can be tested archaeologically but these were not the focus of this thesis. I will discuss the aspects that this thesis has affected. The possibility that population replacement accounts for the Marpole transition has been somewhat changed by this research.

With the current understanding of the regional culture historical sequence (see Figure 7.1), dislocation explanations cannot be accepted. They rely on abrupt shift in the archaeological record at the Locarno Beach - Marpole interface. This abrupt shift does not seem to occur. The early Marpole assemblages of the Old Musqueam subphase are almost indistinguishable from Locarno Beach components. However, this thesis offers new data which opens the door to dislocation. With my newly proposed regional culture historical sequence (see Figure 7.3), dislocation must be re-examined. There is now a more dramatic shift at the Locarno Beach - Marpole transition around 2000 BP. This shift may be the most profound in the Gulf of Georgia during the last 3500 years. If population replacement occurred at all, it occurred at this time.

The dislocation argument is further strengthened by a geographic division with Southern Vancouver Island developing separately from the Fraser River Delta and the Gulf Islands. One possible explanation for the contemporaneous differences noted between the Beach Grove and Garrison subphases on one hand and the Bowker Creek subphase on the other, is that a new population is represented by Beach Grove and Garrison assemblages.

It is the general consensus among Northwest Coast archaeologists that Marpole marks the onset of increased sociocultural complexity predicated on an economy of stored salmon (see Chapter Three). Discontinuity theorists would argue that this major development is indicative of a population replacement. However, there is strong evidence that the process of increased status differential (Carlson and Hobler 1993, Arcas 1991a) and the technology for salmon storage (Matson 1991, Pratt 1991) both predate Marpole. Marpole marks the stage where these processes were intensified, not developed. In this case Marpole may be seen not as innovative, but rather as an intensive expression of the pre-existing knowledge base. Given this argument, the need to explain the rise of sociocultural complexity predicated on intensive salmon storage with population replacement is no longer necessary. Salmon storage and status inequality are not new developments brought with a new population, they both exist but are not widespread in Locarno Beach populations.

In addition, skeletal evidence from Curtin (1999) shows with direct evidence that dislocation across the Locarno Beach - Marpole transition at least in Gabriola Island burials is not taking place. She studied a large sample of Locarno Beach aged burials using multivariate dental and infracranial traits. Curtin (1999) found no biological separation between the Locarno Beach population and later dated populations at False Narrows. Thus, she concludes that the artifactual assemblages differences noted between Locarno Beach and Marpole are not a product of population replacement.

The data in this thesis has opened the door a crack for Burley's (1980, 1983) migration explanation, yet I do not favour this position. I support a synthetic version of the continuity explanation. I cannot completely discount the possibility of dislocation but I feel the shift is better explained using continuity.

The continuity explanations presented in Chapter Three were wide ranging and often only differed in the choice of prime mover. As mentioned previously, little can be said regarding the processes that interconnected the variables in those explanations. This thesis was not designed to test those explanations, if testing is even possible. However, this thesis sheds light on certain aspects of those explanations which I will now discuss.

The continuity explanations describe the Locarno Beach - Marpole transition as a region-wide phenomenon. This thesis has shown that the region is not homogenous and different areas felt the transition differentially, if at all.

The regional culture historical sequence seems to bifurcate around 2000 BP, see Figure 7.3. No current continuity explanation can account for this situation. I will now try to reexamine the continuity explanations to allow for the bifurcation. Explanations of culture change must be flexible enough to account for the variation experienced on Southern Vancouver Island. Some explanations lack that flexibility and can be rejected at this time. Given that Southern Vancouver Island and the Gulf Islands are linked geographically it is unlikely that climate change or other environmental variable can be implicated as a prime mover. It would be hard to argue that there existed noticeable climatic or environmental difference between Saltspring Island and Cadboro Bay that would account for an apparently separate cultural sequence. The direct implication of climatic or environmental change as a prime mover cannot be accepted. Having said that, it becomes possible that the differences noted on Southern Vancouver Island are of a cultural nature.

Differential cultural response to changing region-wide climatic or environmental conditions becomes a conceivable explanation. Indirectly, all of the continuity explanations can be viewed with an eye towards differential cultural response. What is clear about the rise of Marpole is that it is predicated on an intensification of the salmon fishery made possible by storage technology (see Chapter Three). The ability to store salmon is not a new development during this period but the adaptation to invest considerably more time and labour in the technology. This marks the rise of Marpole (Matson 1992, Pratt 1992). The explanations presented in Chapter Three describe that adaptation as the product of resource depletion, territorial circumscription, individual competition and/or the need for increased economic efficiency. Taking parts from all of these explanations, I offer a synthetic view of the Locarno Beach - Marpole transition.

Following Croes and Hackenberger (1988) I feel that population increase during Locarno Beach times led to seasonal resource depletion. This may have been exacerbated by changing climatic trends (Mitchell 1971b). A region-wide response was the gradual shift from a generalized to a more specific subsistence strategy. The Old Musqueam subphase shows this moderate intensification. The subphase is not entirely consistent with Locarno Beach *sensu stricto*, and probably represents this changing realignment of the economy. This is a relatively minor shift in the regional culture history, but the creation of the Old Musqueam subphase sets the stage for the major cultural changes about to happen.

As shown in Figure 6.2, the separation of the Old Musqueam and Bowker Creek cluster from the Beach Grove and Garrison one is dramatic. Arising from the similar basal cultures, the Gulf of Georgia region bifurcates into Marpole on the Fraser River Delta and Gulf Islands and to the Bowker Creek cluster of Locarno Beach on Southern Vancouver Island (see Figure 7.3). If this situation arose from differential cultural response, then to what? and why at this time?

The answer, I believe, is a drastic and rapid depletion in the resource base of the region. A major earthquake, 8.0 or greater on the Richter scale, is thought to have occurred around 2000 BP in the Gulf of Georgia (Mathewes and Clague 1994). Mathewes and Clague (1994) argue that stratigraphy at several non-archaeological sites shows terrestrial peat overlain with intertidal mud and there is also evidence for soil liquefaction at the Serpentine River near Vancouver. Microfossil analysis gives further support to a major earthquake occurring at this time (Mathewes and Clague 1994).

The evidence suggests that this event caused subsidence across the entire Cascadia Subduction Zone (the Southern Gulf of Georgia, from the Lower Mainland to Southern Vancouver Island) with possible effects felt as far away as Southern Washington State (Mathewes and Clague 1994). This earthquake would have adversely affected the resource base with a realignment of the intertidal zones and an increase in brackish environments (Mathewes and Clague 1994). The exact effects on the resource base of the Gulf of Georgia are unknown, however a later event in the Fraser River Canyon may offer some clues.

Hayden and Ryder (1991) have hypothesized that a large landslide possibly caused by an earthquake, probably dammed the Fraser River around 1100 BP. They offer Texas Creek or Jones Bench as possible locations of this obstruction. Hayden and Ryder (1991) feel that the abrupt abandonment of Keatley Creek and other pithouses upstream on the Fraser relates directly to the damming. They feel that a multi-year blockage of the river decimated the salmon fishing economy of the areas upstream forcing the area's inhabitants to relocate. This same event may have lead to culture change downstream in the Gulf of Georgia region at 1100 BP, as this roughly coincides with the transition from Marpole to the Gulf of Georgia culture type.

Returning to the Gulf of Georgia 2000 BP earthquake, some significant differences are noted. A massive long-term blockage is not indicated. The culture histories of the Plateau and Fraser River Canyon do not show sudden culture change at 2000 BP, as the Gulf of Georgia does. Thus the complete decimation of the salmon runs that Hayden and Ryder (1991) feel cause the abandonment of Keatley Creek is not a likely result of the 2000 BP earthquake. However, there may have been significant short-term disruption of the resource base. I will now offer a few possible scenarios that may have been caused by the earthquake.

(1) Region-wide subsidence may have damaged areas of important vegetation. There was a rapid change in vegetation at several locales across the Southern Gulf of Georgia. Freshwater scrubland was transformed into tidal marshes (Mathewes and Clague 1994). Bracken fern and camas may have been detrimentally affected. An increase in brackish environments may have lowered the amount of plant resources available. This may have forced a reliance on the salmon fishery to overcome seasonal shortages in plant foods.

(2) An extensive silting and realignment of intertidal areas may have lowered the number of available shellfish. It is possible that small landslides brought large quantities of silt down the Fraser River and deposited this silt over shellfish beds, drastically lowering the numbers of shellfish. The rapid flooding of low-lying areas may have also increased the amount of silt deposited in intertidal areas (Wigen pers. comm). This process would have been felt primarily in the Fraser River Delta with only minor disruption caused on Southern Vancouver Island.

Subsidence would have also meant that the depth of the current shellfish beds would change. This would have meant that some shellfish beds were no longer available to humans as they were now to deep to exploit. Also it would have meant that with deeper water the temperature would be lower, endangering temperature-sensitive species of shellfish, such as mussels (Wigen pers. comm.). Shellfish would have generally rebounded quickly in any situation. Their swimming larvae would have allowed quick colonization of newly created intertidal zones and after short-term disruption, in the long-term they may have benefited from this earthquake. The temporary shortfall of shellfish however, may have necessitated a shift to intensive salmon storage.

(3) A temporary blockage of the Fraser River may have damaged the salmon fishery. This may have caused the temporary over-reliance on shellfish as "starvation food". Overshellfishing may have then lead to the inability of the resource to recover and a major shellfish population crash is possible. Once the salmon fishery rebounded the lack of shellfish in winter months may have forced the intensification of salmon storage.

(4) It is also possible that a landslide severely damaged the salmon fishery so that almost an entire year's run was decimated. In this instance a cyclical famine or food shortage would occur. Every two or four years, dependent on salmon species, a very low number of salmon would return to spawn. This would force a reliance on stored salmon in good years to compensate for a predictable shortfall in bad years. Kew (1992) notes high cyclical variability in salmon runs in the Fraser River, some of which may still be effects from this or later occurring earthquakes. This scenario relies on trade as a mechanism to convert the surplus salmon of good years into obligation of repayment in bad years. The process of trade would also serve to increase pre-existing status differences as those with control of important trade networks could very quickly gain prestige. This idea is not without precedent on the Northwest Coast (Mitchell 1983).

Whichever the mechanism, the timing of the large earthquake coincides with the rise of Marpole in the Fraser River Delta and Gulf Islands, a cultural shift associated with the intensification of the salmon fishery and reliance on the production of a surplus of stored salmon.

As Schalk (1977) points out, in the Gulf of Georgia, only anadromous fish resources are readily intensifiable without noticeable future degradation of the resource. Other resources would suffer from over-harvesting and would be unable to recover on a yearly basis. Even if the Fraser River fishery was damaged by an earthquake the numbers of available fish during peak times would probably be far beyond human needs.

The technology to preserve salmon was known in Locarno Beach times (Matson 1991, Pratt 1991). It was however not widespread nor intensive. The cultural sequence shows rapid change at around 2000 BP. This change has been associated with the adoption of more intensive and widespread salmon storage. The investment of time and labour prior to Marpole for intensive salmon harvesting made the practice undesirable. It is only when faced with resource depletion and seasonal food scarcity does the benefit of intensive salmon processing outweigh the added investment. Once intensive salmon storage begins the processes alluded to in several of the explanations begin to operate.

If ownership (Matson 1992) or restricted access to resources (Coupland 1985) had developed then over a relatively brief time those groups with more productive resource extraction areas or larger and better organized labour pools could produce large surpluses. As shown in Chapter Three (Figures 3.1, page 44 and 3.2, page 55) these surpluses could be reinvested through trade and potlatch, in competition for labour (Burley 1980, Coupland 1985, Hayden 1994 and others). As with the other continuity explanations the difference is really only in the prime mover. Once the ball starts rolling towards sociocultural complexity it becomes hard to stop. I would argue that the prime mover in the development of Marpole is resource depletion driven intensification exacerbated by a large earthquake.

Southern Vancouver Island requires a different explanation. The above explanation describes the rise of Marpole, but as I have argued, Marpole is not in evidence on Southern Vancouver Island. To explain the separate cultural sequence I also invoke differential cultural response to resource depletion as in the case of the Fraser River. Examining the differences in resource base between Southern Vancouver Island and the mainland offers some interesting clues as to why the areas would differ so greatly. The concentrated abundance of salmon seen in the Fraser River is not paralleled on Southern Vancouver Island. Instead, more diffuse schools of fish on their way to Fraser River were available.

Ethnographically, this required a different technology to harvest the salmon: reef-netting. Reef-netting is a highly complex and composite technology that requires advanced labour organization and technological innovation (Suttles 1951, Burley 1980).
It has been argued (Burley 1983, Kew 1992, Easton 1985) that the technology required for reef-netting is later developing. Burley (1980) follows the general archaeological principle that more complex and composite technologies take longer to develop. Kew (1992) argues that due to the complex technology required for reef-netting and its relatively small distribution the subsistence strategy is late developing.
Easton (1985) attempted to measure the antiquity of reef-netting by the accumulation of net weights at reef-netting sites. His findings, although far from absolute, implicate reef-netting as a Gulf of Georgia culture type innovation. Easton (1985:169) goes further noting that "there is no direct evidence to support the proposition that reef-netting itself has a Marpole origin."

Technology is not the only complex innovation needed for efficient reef-netting, highly specialized labour organization is also required. Reef-netting is essentially a capitalist mode of production (Suttles 1951, Easton 1985). Suttles (1951) has noted that, reef-netting captains and crews were hired on the basis of skill not kin affiliation. This amounts to wage labour which is not predicted to occur prior to the development of a class-based society (Easton 1985).

The processing of the fish for drying also required highly organized labour divisions tied to class. Traditionally women were the processors of the salmon (Suttles 1951). Men's roles were limited to members of the reef-netting crew. The limiting factor to surplus accumulation is not the amount of available fish to catch but rather the amount of available labour to process those fish. Ethnographically, slavery provided the large amount of labour required for surplus salmon storage (Suttles 1951, Easton 1985). This allowed low status males to perform the traditionally female task of fish processing.

Reef-netting may predate class society and slavery however, the ethnographic ability to produce large surpluses is built on the presence of these traits. Without them, reef-netting would not allow inhabitants of Southern Vancouver Island the access to large surpluses available on the Fraser River.

Matson (1992) and Coupland (1985) have argued separately that the ethnographic pattern of owned resource areas develops in Marpole and accounts for the witnessed status differences between people. Groups with access to the areas of highest productivity and consistency become higher status as a result of wealth. Those without access or with access to lower quality, more variable resources remain lower status.

Applying these ideas to Southern Vancouver Island, it is possible to argue the technology and labour organization required for reef-netting had not yet developed. The reason that Southern Vancouver Island remains in Locarno Beach, a more generalized adaptation rather than Marpole, a more specialized one, is that the people of Southern Vancouver Island lacked access to the fish upon which the specialization could occur.

Support for this position comes from the distribution of Marpole and Bowker Creek sites. Mitchell (1971b) separates the two areas into Central and Southern Gulf River Fisherman on the Fraser River and Gulf Islands and the Straits Reef-net Fisherman on Southern Vancouver Island. These boundaries are roughly equivalent to the ethnographic distinction between Straits and Halkomelem speakers. This means that the people of the Gulf Islands are linguistically different form the people on Southern Vancouver Island. Access to the Fraser River fishery was not available to the Straits people; they used reef-netting to obtain salmon (Suttles 1951). If reef-netting does not develop until the Gulf of Georgia culture type then Bowker Creek represents a lag time in technology and/or social organization.

Donald and Mitchell (1975) have shown that areas with more predictable and stable runs have more developed hierarchies. Only with the adoption of reef-netting do the inhabitants of Southern Vancouver Island have stable and predictable access to large quantities of salmon.

Further supporting evidence comes from recent preliminary faunal analysis of Kosapsom (Stewart, n.d.). Marpole has been defined on the basis of an intensive salmon storage subsistence strategy. At Kosapsom I, a Bowker Creek subphase site component, faunal analysis shows that salmon storage is not occurring (Stewart, n.d.). Kosapsom I and hence the Bowker Creek subphase, appear to represent a generalized diet without evidence for stored salmon. Thus the defining feature of Marpole is absent, which speaks to the inability of Southern Vancouver Island inhabitants to procure large quantities of salmon during this time period.

Returning to differential culture response to resource depletion as an explanation, Southern Vancouver Island did not then choose intensification of salmon resources. This coping strategy was unavailable to them. It is probable that the damage of the earthquake affected the Fraser River more than it did the resource base of Southern Vancouver Island. It is possible that less drastic shifts in resource use were needed or that the cultural response is quite simply different than the Fraser River Marpole adaptation. In either case the outcome was that Southern Vancouver Island did not choose or was unable to choose the same intensification strategy as the Fraser River. The clear separation in the cultural sequence with Beach Grove and Garrison contemporaneous with Bowker Creek indicates that the economy of Southern Vancouver Island is markedly different from the Fraser River and Gulf Islands.

This chapter has presented my interpretations of the results of this thesis. My research does not fit well into the currently accepted regional culture historical sequence nor do current explanations of prehistoric culture change explain my results. I have offered a new regional culture history which takes into account the uniqueness of Southern Vancouver Island. I have also proposed a new synthetic continuity explanation which seeks to explain this new culture history and the bifurcation of the Gulf of Georgia during Marpole times. The next and final chapter will summarize this thesis and suggest future research directions.

CHAPTER 8. CONCLUSION

This thesis has looked at an important and oftimes misunderstood time period in British Columbia prehistory. The Marpole culture type marks a significant increase in sociocultural complexity and a host of other cultural characteristics like increased status differentiation, co-operative housing and intensive salmon storage among other traits. The study of the development of Marpole provides an excellent case study for the rise of sociocultural complexity in foraging groups.

This thesis has shown that the process of increased sociocultural complexity is not a simple one. Local factors play a large role in shaping the trajectories of culture change. Much of the Northwest Coast developed similar patterns of sociocultural complexity and it is very apparent from this study that there cannot be an overall general explanation for the creation of the Northwest Coast ethnographic pattern. Many of the same contributing factors, such as resource depletion, population growth and external threat are present in other areas of the Northwest Coast yet local factors must also be taken into account for the timing and nature of each area's culture history.

Multidimensional scaling results from the Gulf of Georgia have shown that this region is not a homogeneous entity. Variation in form across time and space occurs, especially near the Marpole transition. This study upheld the three subphases originally proposed by Matson et al. (1980) and added a new subphase labeled Bowker Creek. This new subphase is comprised entirely of Southern Vancouver Island sites. Bowker Creek is closely related to the Old Musqueam sites but differs greatly from the Beach Grove and Garrison subphase sites. Based on formal, temporal and spatial criteria, I have chosen to assign both the Bowker Creek and Old Musqueam subphases to the Locarno Beach culture type. This reworking the regional culture history has shorted the duration of Marpole to 2000 BP to 1500/1100 BP. Given the results of this thesis, Marpole does not occur on Southern Vancouver Island.

Resource depletion exacerbated by a large earthquake caused the bifurcation of the region into two distinct trajectories of culture history. Differential cultural response to a changing resource base gave birth to Marpole in the Fraser Delta and Gulf Islands while a Locarno Beach subsistence pattern remained on Southern Vancouver Island.

Future Research Directions

This study raises more new questions than it answers. My explanation of this transition, differential cultural response to resource depletion, should be tested further. I have mentioned areas where similar misclassification problems may be occurring (see Chapter Four). It would be invaluable to replicate this study with a site sample from the entire Gulf of Georgia including those with some ambiguity and recently excavated sites.

My explanation relies on the establishment of the ethnographic pattern of resource ownership during Marpole times. To further test this explanation, sites in the four subareas presented by Mitchell (1971b), Northern Gulf Diversified Fishermen, Central and Southern Gulf River Fisherman, Straits Reef-net Fisherman and Puget Sound Diversified Fisherman, should be examined. These subareas represent ethnographic economic patterns, the antiquity of which should be researched.

The earthquake explanation I have proposed needs to be tested. I have offered several possible scenarios whereby a large earthquake could lead to intensification of stored salmon. These ideas need to be further developed. The effects on the resource base for both the Fraser River Delta and Southern Vancouver Island need further research.

Further, the nature of Bowker Creek has not been fully determined. As this thesis did not explicitly set out to study Locarno Beach, the sites chosen did not include many Locarno Beach sites. However, the results show that all of the Southern Vancouver Island sites in this study are Locarno Beach. To properly understand the nature of Bowker Creek within Locarno Beach further study is needed. All that I can say is that Bowker Creek is associated with Locarno Beach but the nature of that association is unknown.

Future research should include sites of Old Musqueam, Bowker Creek and Locarno Beach age. In an upcoming paper, R.G. Matson (n.d.) tackles part of this problem. He uses multidimensional scaling to examine the relationship between Old Musqueam and Locarno Beach. He has included the Bowker Creek and Willows Beach sites as Locarno Beach components. Interestingly enough Bowker Creek and Willows Beach cluster separately from the other components, reinforcing the distinct nature of the Bowker Creek cluster I discovered.

Much more work is needed to fully understand the Locarno Beach - Marpole transition. This time period represents the achievement of not only many of the hallmarks of the Northwest Coast cultural pattern but the rise of sociocultural complexity. These topics are important to archaeologists and anthropologists alike and are worthy of intense future consideration.

REFERENCES CITED

Abbott, Donald N. 1972 The Utility of the Concept of Phase in the Archaeology of the Southern Northwest Coast. *Syesis* 5: 267-78.

Ames, Kenneth M. 1979 Stable and Resilient Systems Along the Skeena River: the Gitskan/Carrier Boundary. In *Skeena River Prehistory*. R. Inglis and G. MacDonald eds. Ottawa: Archaeological Survey of Canada, Mercury Series 87:219-239.

Ames, Kenneth M. 1981 The Evolution of Social Ranking. *American Antiquity* 46:789-805.

Ames, Kenneth M. 1983 Towards a General Model of the Evolution of Ranking Among Foragers. In *The Evolution of Maritime Cultures on the Northeast and the Northwest Coasts of America*. R. J. Nash, ed. Burnaby: Simon Fraser University, Department of Archaeology, Publication no. 11. Pp. 173-184.

Ames, Kenneth M. 1985 Hierarchies, Stress, and Logistical Strategies Among Hunter-gatherers in Northwestern North America. In *Prehistoric Hunter-gatherers: The Emergence of Cultural Complexity*. T.D. Price and J. Brown eds. New York: Academic Press. Pp. 155-180.

Ames, Kenneth M. 1995 Chiefly Power and Household Production on the Northwest Coast. In *Foundations of Social Inequality*. T.D. Price and G.M. Feinman, eds. New York: Plenum Press. Pp. 155-188.

Anderberg, M.P. 1973 *Cluster Analysis for Applications*. San Diego: Academic Press.

Apland, Brian 1981 *Archaeological Salvage Excavation at DgRv 9-Valdes Island*. Report on file, Culture Library, Ministry of Small Business, Tourism and Culture, Victoria.

Arcas Consulting Archaeologists 1991a *Archaeological Investigations at the Little Beach Site, Ucluelet, B.C.* Report on file, Culture Library, Ministry of Small Business, Tourism and Culture, Victoria.

Arcas Consulting Archaeologists *1991b Archaeological Investigations at Tsawwassen, B.C., Volume I, Introduction*. Report on file, Culture Library, Ministry of Small Business, Tourism and Culture, Victoria.

Ball, Bruce F. 1979 *Archaeological Investigation of the Beach Grove Site: A Site Evaluation*. Report on file, Culture Library, Ministry of Small Business, Tourism and Culture, Victoria.

Barnett, Homer 1938 The Coast Salish of Canada. *American Anthropologist* 40(1): 349-58.

Barnett, Homer 1939 Culture Element Distributions, IX: Gulf of Georgia Salish. *University of California Anthropological Records* 1(5):221-95.

Barnett, Homer 1955 *The Coast Salish of British Columbia*. University of Oregon Monographs. Studies in Anthropology 4, Eugene.

Baxter, M. 1994 *Exploratory Multivariate Analysis in Archaeology*. Edinburgh: Edinburgh University Press.

Beattie, Owen B. 1985 A Note on Early Cranial Studies from the Gulf of Georgia Region: Long-heads, Broad-heads and the Myth of Migration. *B.C. Studies*. 66(Summer):28-36.

Bernick, Kathryn 1989 *Water Hazard (DgRs 30) Artifact Recovery Project Report*. Report on file, Culture Library, Ministry of Small Business, Tourism and Culture, Victoria.

Blacklaws, R. 1978 *Excavations at Esquimalt Lagoon: A Contribution to Straits Salish Prehistory*. Unpublished Master's thesis, Department of Archaeology, Simon Fraser University, Burnaby.

Boas, Franz 1889 Notes on the Snanaimuq. *American Anthropologist*. 2(4):321-8.

Boas, Franz 1890 The Lkungen. *Report of the British Association for the Advancement of Science* 60:563-82.

Boas, Franz 1894 *The Indian Tribes of the Lower Fraser River*. London: Spottiswoode.

Boas, Franz 1909 The Kwakiutl of Vancouver Island. *Publications of the Jesup North Pacific Expedition* 5(2):301-522.

Boehm, S. Gay 1973 *Cultural and Non-cultural Variation in the Artifact and Faunal Samples from the St. Mungo Cannery Site, DgRr 2*. Unpublished Master's thesis, Department of Anthropology, University of Victoria.

Borden, Charles E. 1950 Preliminary Report on Archaeological Investigations in the Fraser Delta Region. *Anthropology in British Columbia* 1:13-27.

Borden, Charles E. 1951 Facts and Problems of Northwest Coast Prehistory. *Anthropology in British Columbia* 2:35-52.

Borden, Charles E. 1952 A Uniform Site Designation System for Canada. Anthropology in British Columbia 3:44-48.

Borden, Charles E. 1954 Some Aspects of Prehistoric Coastal-Interior Relations in the Pacific Northwest. *Anthropology in British Columbia* 4:26-32.

Borden, Charles E. 1960 DjRi3, An Early Site in the Fraser Canyon, British Columbia. In *Contributions to Anthropology 1957*. Ottawa: Anthropological Series 45, National Museum of Canada, Bulletin 162, Pp. 101-118.

Borden, Charles E. 1962 West Coast Crossties With Alaska. In *Prehistoric Cultural Relations Between the Arctic and Temperate Zones in North America*. Montreal: Arctic Institute of North America, Technical Paper 11.

Borden, Charles E. 1968a Prehistory of the Lower Mainland. In *Lower Fraser Valley: Evolution of a Cultural Landscape*. Alfred H. Siemens, ed. Vancouver: University of British Columbia Geographical Series 9, Pp. 9-26.

Borden, Charles 1968b A Late Pleistocene Pebble Tool Industry of Southwestern British Columbia. *In Early Man in Western North America*. C. Irwin-Williams, ed. Portales: New Mexico University. Pp. 55-69.

Borden, Charles E. 1970 Culture History of the Fraser Delta Region: An Outline. *B.C. Studies*. Special Issue, 6-7:95-112.

Borden, Charles E. 1975 *Origin and Development of Early Northwest Coast Culture to About 3000 BC*. Ottawa: National Museum of Man, Mercury Series, Archaeological Survey of Canada, Paper no. 45.

Borden, Charles E. 1976 A Water Saturated Site on the Southern Mainland Cost of British Columbia. In *The Excavation of Water-saturated Sites (Wet Sites) on the Northwest Coast of North America*. Ed. D. Croes. Ottawa: National Museum of Man, Mercury Series, Archaeological Survey of Canada Paper no. 50, Pp. 234-60.

Borden, Charles E. and David Archer 1974 Archaeological Salvage at Musqueam Northeast (DhRt 4), Vancouver, British Columbia. In *Archaeological Salvage Projects 1973*. Compiled by W.J. Bryne. Ottawa: National Museum of Man, Mercury Series, Archaeological Survey of Canada Paper no. 50, Pp. 6-11.

Brolly, Richard 1996 *Archaeological Investigations at the Beach Grove Site (DgRs1), Tsawwassen, B.C.* Report on file, Culture Library, Ministry of Small Business, Tourism and Culture, Victoria.

Burley, David V. *1979 Marpole: Anthropological Reconstructions of a Prehistoric Northwest Coast Culture Type*. Unpublished Ph.D. dissertation, Department of Archaeology, Simon Fraser University, Burnaby, B.C.

Burley, David V. 1980 *Marpole: Anthropological Reconstructions of a Prehistoric Northwest Coast Culture Type*. Burnaby: Simon Fraser University, Department of Archaeology Publication no. 8.

Burley, David V. 1981 Inter-regional Exchange in the Gulf of Georgia During the Marpole Phase, 490 BC to AD 500. In *Networks of the Past: Regional Interaction in Archaeology*. Peter Francis et al., eds. Proceedings of the Twelfth Annual Chacmool Conference, The Archaeological Association of the University of Calgary.

Burley, David V. 1983 Cultural Complexity and Evolution in the Development of Coastal Adaptations Among the Micmac and Coast Salish. In *The Evolution of Maritime Cultures on the Northeast and the Northwest Coasts of America*. R. J. Nash, ed. Burnaby: Simon Fraser University, Department of Archaeology Publication no. 11. Pp. 157-172.

Burley, David V. 1989 *Senewe'lets: Culture History of the Nanaimo Coast Salish and the False Narrows Midden*. Victoria: Royal British Columbia Museum no. 2.

Burley, David and Owen Beattie 1987 Coast Salish Origins: Ethnicity and Time Depth in Northwest Coast Prehistory. In *Ethnicity and Culture*. R. Auger et al. Eds. Calgary: 199-207.

Burley, David and Christopher Knusel 1989 Burial Patterns and Archaeological Interpretation: Problems in the Recognition of Ranked Society in the Coast Salish Region. In *Development of Hunting-fishing-gathering Maritime Societies Along the West Coast of North America*. B. Onat, ed. Reprint Proceedings, Vol. IIIC, the Circum-Pacific Prehistory Conference, Seattle, WA, Aug. 1-6, 1989.

Butler, Virginia 1983 *Fish Remains from the Black River Sites (45K159 and 45K151-D)*. Unpublished Master's thesis, Department of Anthropology, University of Washington, Seattle.

Calvert, S. Gay 1970 The St. Mungo Cannery Site: A Preliminary Report. In Archaeology in British Columbia: New Discoveries. R. Carlson, ed. *B.C. Studies* Special Issue 6-7:54-76.

Capes, Katherine H. 1977 Archaeological Investigations of the Millard Creek Site, Vancouver Island, British Columbia. *Syesis* 10:57-84.

Carlson, Roy 1960 Chronology and Culture Change in the San Juan Islands, Washington. *American Antiquity* 25(4):562-86.

Carlson, Roy 1970 Excavations at Helen Point on Mayne Island. *B.C. Studies* Special Issue 6-7:113-125.

Carlson, Roy 1983 Method and Theory in Northwest Coast Archaeology. *In The Evolution of Maritime Cultures on the Northeast and the Northwest Coasts of America*. R. J. Nash, ed. Burnaby: Simon Fraser University, Department of Archaeology Publication no. 11. Pp.27-40.

Carlson, Roy 1986 *The 1985 Excavations at the Canal Site (DeRt 1 and DeRt 2)*. Report on file, Culture Library, Ministry of Small Business, Tourism and Culture, Victoria.

Carlson, Roy 1987 Cultural and Ethnic Continuity on the Pacific Coast of British Columbia. Paper presented at the 16th Pacific Sciences Conference, Seoul.

Carlson, Roy 1990a History of Research in Archaeology. In *Handbook of North American Indians, vol. 7*, Northwest Coast. Wayne Suttles, vol. ed. Washington Smithsonian Institution.

Carlson, Roy 1990b *The 1986 Excavations at the Canal Site (DeRt 1 and DeRt 2)*. Report on file, Culture

Library, Ministry of Small Business, Tourism and Culture, Victoria.

Carneiro, Robert 1970 A Theory of the Origin of the State. In *The Transition to Statehood in the New World*. G. Jones and R. Kautz, eds. Cambridge: Cambridge University Press.

Charlton, Arthur 1980 *The Belcarra Park Site*. Simon Fraser University, Department of Archaeology, Publication no 9.

Chatters, James C. 1989 The Antiquity of Economic Differentiation Within Households in the Puget Sound Region, Northwest Coast. in *Households and Communities*. S. MacEachern, D. Archer and R. Garvin, eds. Calgary: University of Calgary Archaeological Association, Pp. 168-78.

Clark, Brenda 1984 *Quick's Pond: The Analysis of a Surface Collection from a Microblade Site on the Saanich Peninsula, Vancouver Island*. Victoria: Royal British Columbia Museum.

Coates, Clinton 1994 *Emergency Monitoring of Domestic Gas Installation for 2452 Esplanade, Willows Beach Site (DcRt 10)*. Report on file, Culture Library, Ministry of Small Business, Tourism and Culture, Victoria.

Coupland, Gary 1985 Restricted Access, Resource Control and the Evolution of Status Inequality Among Hunter-Gatherers. In *Status, Structure and Stratification*. M. Thompson et al. Eds. Calgary: University of Calgary Archaeological Association. Pp. 217-226.

Coupland, Gary 1988 *Prehistoric Cultural Change at Kitselas Canyon*. Archaeological Survey of Canada, Mercury Series no. 138.

Coupland, Gary 1991 The Point Grey Site: A Marpole Spring Village Component. *Canadian Journal of Archaeology* 15:73-96.

Croes, Dale R. 1976 *The Excavation of Water-saturated Sites (Wet Sites) on the Northwest Coast of North America*. Ottawa: National Museum of Man, Mercury Series, Archaeological Survey of Canada Paper no. 50.

Croes, Dale R. 1987 Locarno Beach at Hoko River, Olympic Peninsula, Washington: Makah/Nootkan, Salishan, Chimakuan or Who? In *Ethnicity and Culture*. R. Auger & M.F. Glass, eds. Proceedings of the 18th Annual Chacmool Conference, University of Calgary, Pp. 259-283.

Croes, Dale R. 1988 The Significance of the 3000 BP Hoko River Waterlogged Fishing Camp in Our Understanding of Southern Northwest Coast Cultural Evolution. In *Wetsite Archaeology*. Barbara A. Purdy, ed. Caldwell, NJ: Telford Press.

Croes, Dale R. 1989 Prehistoric Ethnicity on the Northwest Coast of North America: An Evaluation of Style in Basketry and Lithics. *Journal of Anthropological Archaeology*. 8:101-130.

Croes, Dale R. 1992 Exploring Prehistoric Subsistence Change on the Northwest Coast. In *Research in Economic Anthropology*, Suppl 6. Dale Croes, Rebecca Hawkins and Barry Isaac eds. Greenwich, CT: JAI Press, Pp. 337-366.

Croes, Dale R. and Steven Hackenberger 1988 Hoko River Archaeological Complex. In *Modeling Prehistoric Northwest Coast Economic Evolution in Prehistoric Economies of the Pacific Northwest Coast, Research in Economic Anthropology*, Suppl. 3. Barry Isaac, ed., Greenwich, CT.:JAI Press, Pp. 19-85.

Curtin, Joanne 1999 Biological Relationships at the Locarno/Marpole Transition: The Evidence from Gabriola Island. *The Midden*. 31(2): 3-4.

Curtin, Joanne, Mark Finnis and Morley Eldridge 1991 *A Human Burial from the Willows Beach Site, DcRt 10*. Report on file, Culture Library, Ministry of Small Business, Tourism and Culture, Victoria.

Cybulski, Jerome S. 1991 Observations of Labret Wear, Appendix I. In *1989 and 1990 Crescent Beach Excavations, Final Report*. Report on file, Culture Library, Ministry of Small Business, Tourism and Culture, Victoria.

Donald, Leland 1985 On the Possibility of Social Class in Societies Based on Extractive Subsistence. In *Status, Structure and Stratification: Current Archaeological Reconstructions*. M. Thompson, M.T. Garcia and F. Kense, eds. Calgary: University of Calgary Archaeological Association. Pp 237-244.

Donald, Leland and Donald Mitchell 1975 Some Correlates of Local Group Rank Among the Southern Kwakiutl. *Ethnology*. 14:325-46.

Drucker, Philip 1943 *Archaeological Survey of the Northern Northwest Coast*. Anthropological Papers 20. Bureau of American Ethnology Bulletin 133.

Drucker, Philip 1955 *Indians of the Northwest Coast*. New York: Natural History Press.

Drucker, Philip 1958 Sources of Northwest Coast Culture. In *New Interpretation of Aboriginal American Culture History*. Betty Meggers, ed. Washington, DC: Anthropological Society of Washington, Pp. 59-81.

Duff, Wilson 1956 *Unique Stone Artifacts From the Gulf Islands*. Provincial Museum of Natural History and Anthropology. Report for the Year 1955. Victoria: British Columbia Provincial Museum, Pp. 45-55.

Easton, Norman 1985 *The Underwater Archaeology of Straits Salish Reef-netting*. Unpublished Master's thesis, Department of Anthropology, University of Victoria.

Eldridge, Morley 1987a *Construction Monitoring and Emergency Salvage Excavation at 2368 Esplanade, Oak Bay, B.C. (DcRt 10, the Willows*

Beach Archaeological Site). Report on file, Culture Library, Ministry of Small Business, Tourism and Culture, Victoria.

Eldridge, Morley 1987b *Archaeological Monitoring and Salvage Excavation at the Willows Beach Site, DcRt 10, Oak Bay, B.C.* Report on file, Culture Library, Ministry of Small Business, Tourism and Culture, Victoria.

Eldridge, Morley 1990 *Willows Beach, DcRt 10: Impact Assessment of the East Coast Interceptor.* Report on file, Culture Library, Ministry of Small Business, Tourism and Culture, Victoria.

Eldridge, Morley 1992a *Archaeological Mitigation for the East Coast Interceptor, Willows Beach, Oak Bay (DcRt 10) and other Locations.* Report on file, Culture Library, Ministry of Small Business, Tourism and Culture, Victoria.

Eldridge, Morley 1992b *Monitoring of House Construction at 3905C Cadboro Bay Road, DcRt-15.* Report on file, Culture Library, Ministry of Small Business, Tourism and Culture, Victoria.

Eldridge, Morley and Mark Finnis 1991 *Archaeological Monitoring of Gas Pipeline Construction on the Esplanade at the Willows Beach Site, DcRt 10.* Report on file, Culture Library, Ministry of Small Business, Tourism and Culture, Victoria.

Fladmark, Knut 1975 *A Paleoecological Model for Northwest Coast Prehistory.* Ottawa: National Museum of Man, Mercury Series, Archaeological Survey of Canada Paper no. 43.

Fried, Morton 1967 *The Evolution of Political Society.* New York: Random House.

Gaston, Jeanette L. 1975 *The Extension of the Fraser Delta Cultural Sequence into Northwest Washington.* Unpublished Master's thesis, Western Washington State College, Bellingham.

Grabert, Garland and Curtis Larson 1975 Marine Transgressions and Cultural Adaptations: Preliminary Tests of an Environmental Model. In *Prehistoric Maritime Adaptations in the Circumpolar Zone.* W. Fitzhugh, ed. The Hague: Mouton. Pp 229-251.

Haggarty, James and John Sendey 1976 *Test Excavations at Georgeson Bay, British Columbia.* British Columbia Provincial Museum Occasional Papers no. 19. Victoria: British Columbia Provincial Museum.

Hall, Roberta and James Haggarty 1981 Human Skeletal Remains and Associated Cultural Material from the Hill Site, DfRu 4, Saltspring Island, British Columbia. In *Contributions to Physical Anthropology, 1978-1980.* J.S. Cybulski, ed. National Museum of Man, Mercury Series, Archaeological Survey of Canada Paper No. 106, Ottawa. Pp. 64-106.

Ham, Leonard 1982 *Seasonality, Shell Midden Layers and Coast Salish Subsistence Activities at Crescent Beach, DgRr 1.* Unpublished Ph.D. dissertation, Department of Anthropology and Sociology, University of British Columbia, Vancouver.

Hanson, Diane 1990 Prehistoric Subsistence at the Pender Canal Sites and the Surrounding Area. *Northwest Anthropological Research Notes* 24:195-212.

Hayden, Brian 1994 Competition, Labour and Complex Hunter-Gatherers. In *Key Issues in Hunter-Gatherer Research.* E.S. Burch and L.J. Ellana, eds. Oxford: Berg. 223-239.

Hayden, Brian 1995 Pathways to Power: Principles for Creating Socioeconomic Inequalities. In *Foundations of Social Inequality.* T.D. Price and G.M. Feinman, eds. New York: Plenum Press. Pp. 15-86.

Hayden, Brian and June M. Ryder 1991 Prehistoric Cultural Collapse in the Lillooet Area. *American Antiquity.* 56(1): 50-65.

Hayden, Nancy I. *1967 Summary of the 1967 Excavation at DcRt-15, Cadboro Bay.* Report on file, Culture Library, Ministry of Small Business, Tourism and Culture, Victoria.

Hill-Tout, Charles 1895 Later Prehistoric Man in British Columbia. *Transactions of the Royal Society of Canada 2nd Series*, 1(2):103-122, Ottawa.

Hill-Tout, Charles 1903 Ethnological Studies of the Mainland Halkomelem, a *Division of the Salish of British Columbia in 72nd Report of the British Association for the Advancement of Science for 1902.*

Hill-Tout, Charles 1904 Ethnological Report on the Stseelis and Sk aults Tribes of the Halkomelem Division of the Salish of British Columbia. *Journal of the Anthropological Institute of Great Britain and Ireland* 34:311-76.

Hill-Tout, Charles 1905 Some Features of the Language and Culture of the Salish. *American Anthropologist* 7(4):674-87.

Hill-Tout, Charles 1907 Report on the Ethnology of the South-eastern Tribes of Vancouver Island, British Columbia. *Journal of the Royal Anthropological Institute of Great Britain and Ireland* 37:306-74.

Hill-Tout, Charles 1948 *The Great Fraser Midden.* Vancouver: Vancouver Art, Historical and Scientific Association.

Hodson, F.R., Peter Sneath and John Doran 1966 Some Experiments in the Numerical Analysis of Archaeological Data. *Biometrika* 53:311-324.

Jenness, Diamond n.d. *The Saanich Indians of Vancouver Island.* (manuscript no. VII-G-8M). Ottawa: Canadian Ethnographic Service Archives, National Museum of Civilization.

Johnstone, Dave 1991 *The Function(s) of a Shell Midden Site from the Southern Strait of Georgia.* Unpublished Master's thesis, Department of Archaeology, Simon Fraser University, Burnaby.

Jorgensen, Joseph 1969 *Salish Language and Culture: A Statistical Relationship of Internal Relationships, History and Evolution.* Language Science Monographs 3 Bloomington: Indiana University.

Jorgensen, Joseph 1980 *Western Indians.* San Francisco :WH Freeman and Co.

Keddie, Grant 1984 Fortified Defensives Sites and Burial Cairns of the Songhees Indians. *The Midden.* 16(4) 7-9.

Keddie, Grant 1987 *Salvage Excavations in Northwest Cadboro Bay Archaeological Site, DcRt-9.* Report on file, Culture Library, Ministry of Small Business, Tourism and Culture, Victoria.

Keddie, Grant n.d. *The Early Human History of the Gorge Waterway.* Unpublished manuscript.

Kenny, Ray 1971 *Preliminary Report: Willows Beach Excavation, June-August 1971.* Report on file, Culture Library, Ministry of Small Business, Tourism and Culture, Victoria.

Kenny, Ray 1974 *Archaeological Investigations at the Willows Beach Site, Southeastern Vancouver Island.* Unpublished Master's thesis, Department of Archaeology, University of Calgary.

Kew, Michael 1992 Salmon Availability, Technology, and Cultural Adaptation in the Fraser River Watershed. In *A Complex Culture of the British Columbia Plateau.* B. Hayden, ed. Vancouver: University of British Columbia Press. Pp 177-221.

Kidd, Robert 1969 The Archaeology of the Fossil Bay Site, Sucia Island, Northwestern Washington State, in *Relation to the Fraser Delta Sequence.* Paper No. 2, Contributions to Anthropology VII: Archaeology, National Museums of Canada, Bulletin 232, Ottawa.

King, Arden 1950 Cattle Point, A Stratified Site on the Southern Northwest Coast. *Memoirs of the Society for American Archaeology* 7.

Kornbacher, Kimberly 1989 *Shell Midden Lithic Technology: An Investigation of Change at British Camp (45SJ24), San Juan Island.* Unpublished Master's thesis, Department of Anthropology and Sociology, University of British Columbia, Vancouver.

Kroeber, Alfred L. 1939 *Cultural and Natural Areas of North America.* Berkeley: University of California Publications in American Archaeology and Ethnology no. 38.

Kruskal, Joseph, B. 1964 Multidimensional Scaling by Optimizing Goodness of Fit to a Nonmetric Hypothesis. *Psychometrika.* 29:1-27.

Krukal, Joseph, B and Myron Wish 1978 *Multidimensional Scaling.* Beverly Hills: Sage.

McMillan, Alan 1998 Changing View of Nuu-Cah-Nulth Culture History: Evidence of Population Replacement in Barkley Sound. *Canadian Journal of Archaeology* 22(1):5-18.

McMillan, Alan and Denis St. Claire 1982 *Alberni Prehistory: Archaeological and Ethnographic Investigations on Western Vancouver Island.* Theytus Books and Alberni Valley Museum, Penticton and Port Alberni.

McMurdo, A. 1976 *Excavations at Maple Bank Site, DcRu 12.* Report on file, Culture Library, Ministry of Small Business, Tourism and Culture, Victoria.

McMurdo, John 1974 *The Archaeology of Helen Point, Mayne Island.* Unpublished Master's thesis, Department of Archaeology, Simon Fraser University.

Matson, R.G. 1974 Clustering and Scaling of Gulf of Georgia Sites. *Syesis* 7:101-14.

Matson, R.G. 1976 *The Glenrose Cannery Site.* Ottawa: National Museum of Man, Mercury Series, Archaeological Survey Papers 52.

Matson, R.G. 1981 Prehistoric Subsistence Patterns in the Fraser Delta: The Evidence from the Glenrose Cannery Site. *B.C. Studies.* 48: 64-85.

Matson, R.G. 1983 Intensification and the Development of Cultural Complexity: The Northwest Versus the Northeast Coast. In *The Evolution of Maritime Cultures on the Northeast and the Northwest Coasts of America.* R. J. Nash, ed. Burnaby: Simon Fraser University, Department of Archaeology Publication no. 11. Pp. 125-148.

Matson, R.G. 1985 The Relationship Between Sedentism and Status Inequalities Among Hunters and Gatherers. In *Status, Structure and Stratification.* M. Thompson et al. Eds. Calgary: University of Calgary Archaeological Association. Pp. 245-252.

Matson, R.G. 1989 The Locarno Beach Phase and the Origins of the Northwest Coast Pattern. In *Development of Hunting-fishing-gathering Maritime Societies Along the West Coast of North America.* Ed. By B. Onat. The Circum-Pacific Prehistory Conference, Seattle, Aug. 1989. Pullman: Washington State University Press.

Matson, R.G. 1992 The Evolution of Northwest Coast Subsistence. *In Research in Economic Anthropology*, Suppl. 6, Long Term Subsistence Change in Prehistoric North America. Eds. Dale Croes, R. Hawkins and B. Isaac. Greenwich, CT:JAI Press, Pp.. 367-428.

Matson, R.G. n.d. *The Place of the Locarno Beach Culture in the Development of the Ethnographic Northwest Coast Cultures.* Unpublished manuscript in author's possession.

Matson, R.G. n.d. Tscale. Computer program.

Matson, R.G. and Gary Coupland 1995 *The Prehistory of the Northwest Coast.* San Diego: Academic Press.

Matson, R.G., D. Ludowicz and W. Boyd 1980 *Excavations at Beach Grove in 1980.* Report on file, Culture Library, Ministry of Small Business, Tourism and Culture, Victoria.

Matson, R.G., H. Pratt and L. Rankin 1991 *1989 and 1990 Crescent Beach Excavations, Final Report*. Report on file, Culture Library, Ministry of Small Business, Tourism and Culture, Victoria.

Matson, R.G. and D.L. True 1974 Site Relationships at Quebrada Tarapaca, Chile: A Comparison of Clustering and Scaling Techniques. *American Antiquity* 39(1):51-73.

Matthewes, Rolf W. 1973 A Palynological Study of Postglacial Vegetation Changes in the University Research Forest, Southwestern British Columbia. *Canadian Journal of Botany* 51(2): 2085-2103.

Matthewes, Rolf W. and John J. Clague 1994 Detection of Large Prehistoric Earthquakes in the Pacific Northwest by Microfossil Analysis. *Science* 264:686-691.

Mitchell, Donald H. 1968a Microblades: A Long Standing Gulf of Georgia Tradition. *American Antiquity* 33:11-15.

Mitchell, Donald H. 1968b Excavations at Two Trench Embankments in The Gulf of Georgia Region. *Syesis* Vol. 3, 29-46.

Mitchell, Donald H. 1971a The Dionisio Point Site and Gulf Island Culture History. *Syesis* Vol. 4, 145-68.

Mitchell, Donald H. 1971b Archaeology of the Gulf of Georgia Area, A Natural Region and Its Culture Types. *Syesis*. 4 (Suppl. 1).

Mitchell, Donald H. 1974 Salvage Excavations at site DfSf 13, Buckley Bay, British Columbia. In *Archaeological Salvage Projects 1973*. W.J. Byrne, ed. National Museum of Man, Mercury Series, Archaeological Survey of Canada Paper No. 26, Ottawa. Pp. 88-92.

Mitchell, Donald H. 1979 Bowker Creek: A Microblade Site on Southeastern Vancouver Island. *Syesis* 12:77-100.

Mitchell, Donald H. 1983 Tribes and Chiefdoms of the Northwest Coast: The Tsimshian Case. In *The Evolution of Maritime Cultures on the Northeast and Northwest Coasts of America*. R.J. Nash, ed. Burnaby: Simon Fraser University Press. Pp. 57-64.

Mitchell, Donald H. 1986 *Report on the 1985 Activities of the DcRt 10 Screening Project*. Report on file, Culture Library, Ministry of Small Business, Tourism and Culture, Victoria.

Mitchell, Donald H. 1988a Changing Patterns of Resource Use in the Prehistory of Queen Charlotte Strait, British Columbia. In *Research in Economic Anthropology*, Suppl. 3: Prehistoric Economies of the Pacific Northwest Coast. Barry Isaac, ed. Greenwich, CT: JAI Press. Pp. 245-290.

Mitchell, Donald H. 1988b The J. Puddleduck Site: A Northern Strait of Georgia Locarno Beach Component and its Predecessor. *Contribution to Human History No. 2* Victoria: Royal British Columbia Museum.

Mitchell, Donald H. 1989 Changing Fortunes: Kwakiutl-Salish Frontiers of the Central Northwest Coast. Development of Maritime Societies Along the West Coast of North America, Circum-Pacific Prehistory Conference. Seattle.

Mitchell, Donald H. 1990 Prehistory of the Coasts of Southern British Columbia and Northern Washington. In *Handbook of North American Indians, vol. 7, Northwest Coast*. Wayne Suttles, vol. ed. Washington: Smithsonian Institution.

Mitchell, Donald H. 1995 *Excavations at Kosapsom Park (DcRu4) Saanich, 1994*. Report on file, Culture Library, Ministry of Small Business, Tourism and Culture, Victoria.

Mitchell, Donald H. 1996 *Excavations at Kosapsom Park (DcRu4) Saanich, 1995*. Report on file, Culture Library, Ministry of Small Business, Tourism and Culture, Victoria.

Monks, Gregory 1976 Quantitative Comparison of Glenrose Components with the Marpole Component from Site DhRt 3. In *The Glenrose Cannery Site*. R.G. Matson, ed. National Museum of Man, Mercury Series, Archaeological Survey of Canada Paper no. 52, Ottawa. Pp 267-280.

Monks, Gregory 1977 *An Examination of Relationships Between Artifact Classes and Food Resource Remains at Deep Bay, DiSe 7*. Unpublished Ph.D. dissertation, Department of Anthropology and Sociology, University of British Columbia, Vancouver.

Monks, Gregory 1987 Prey as Bait: The Deep Bay Example. *Canadian Journal of Archaeology* 11:119-42.

Morgan, Lewis Henry 1877 *Ancient Society*. New York: World Publishing.

Morgan, Vera E. 1996 *Results of Cultural Resource Survey and testing for the Washington State Department of Transportation's Planned SR 101 Sequim bypass project, Clallam County, Washington*. Eastern Washington University Reports in Archaeology and History 100-92, Archaeological and Historical Services, Eastern Washington University, Cheney, WA.

Morgan, Vera E. 1998 The Locarno Beach Component at Site 45CA426, Sequim, Washington. paper presented at Canadian Archaeological Association Conference Victoria 98. Victoria, B.C., May 9.

Morgan, Vera E. 1999 *The SR-101 Sequim Bypass Archaeological Project: Mid- to Late-Holocene Occupations on the Northern Olympic, Clallam County, Washington., Volume 1*. Eastern Washington University reports in Archaeology and History 100-108, Archaeological and Historical Services, Cheney, WA.

Murray, Rebecca 1982 *Analysis of Artifacts from Four Duke Point Area Sites Near Nanaimo, B.C.: An Example of Cultural Continuity in the Southern Gulf of Georgia Region*. National Museum of Man, Mercury Series, Archaeological Survey of Canada Paper No. 113, Ottawa.

Nash, Ronald J., ed. 1983 *The Evolution of Maritime Cultures on the Northeast and the Northwest Coasts of America*. Burnaby: Simon Fraser University, Department of Archaeology Publication no. 11.

Nordquist, Delmar 1976 45SN100- The Biederbost Site, Kidd's Duval Site. In *The Excavation of Water-saturated Sites (Wet Sites) on the Northwest Coast of North Coast of North America*. D. Croes, ed. National Museum of Man, Mercury Series, Archaeological Survey of Canada Paper No. 50, Ottawa. Pp. 186-200.

Osbourne, Douglas, Warren Caldwell and Robert Crabtree 1956 Evidence of the Early Lithic in the Pacific Northwest. *Research Studies of the State College of Washington* 24:38-44.

Owens, D'Ann, Morley Eldridge, Marjorie Dunlop, Robbin Chatan and John Maxwell 1996 *Vancouver Island Highway Project, Victoria Approaches Archaeological Inventory and Impact Assessment*. Report on file, Culture Library, Ministry of Small Business, Tourism and Culture, Victoria.

Owens, D'Ann, John Maxwell, Josalyn Ferguson, Rob Vincent and Peter Dady 1997 *Vancouver Island Highway Project, Victoria Approaches Archaeological Data Recovery DcRu-572*. Report on file, Culture Library, Ministry of Small Business, Tourism and Culture, Victoria.

Patenaude, Valerie 1985 *Pitt River Archaeological Site: A Coast Salish Seasonal Camp on the Lower Fraser River*. Report on file, Culture Library, Ministry of Small Business, Tourism and Culture, Victoria.

Peacock, William 1982 *The Telep Site: A Late Autumn Fish Camp of the Locarno Beach Culture Type*. Report on file, Culture Library, Ministry of Small Business, Tourism and Culture, Victoria.

Peacock, Sandra *1998 Putting Down Roots: The Emergence of Wild Plant Food Production on the Canadian Plateau*. Unpublished Ph.D. dissertation, Department of Geography, University of Victoria, Victoria.

Pearson, Gordon and Minze Stuiver 1986 High -Precision Calibration of the Radiocarbon Time Scale, 500-2500 BC *Radiocarbon* 28 (2B):839-862.

Percy, Richard 1974 *The Prehistoric Cultural Sequence at Crescent Beach, British Columbia*. Unpublished Master's thesis, Department of Archaeology, Simon Fraser University, Burnaby.

Pollit, J. and Gregory Monks 1970 *Project Report: DcRt 10*. Report on file, Culture Library, Ministry of Small Business, Tourism and Culture, Victoria.

Powell, G. Robert 1979 *Archaeological in the Victoria Region*. Report on file, Culture Library, Ministry of Small Business, Tourism and Culture, Victoria.

Pratt, Heather *1991 Locarno Beach Site Artifact Classifcation. 1989 and 1990 Crescent Beach Excavations, Final Report*. Matson, R.G., H. Pratt and L. Rankin, eds. Report on file, Culture Library, Ministry of Small Business, Tourism and Culture, Victoria.

Pratt, Heather 1992 *The Charles Culture of the Gulf of Georgia: A Reevaluation of the Charles Culture and its Three Subphases*. Unpublished Master's thesis, Department of Anthropology and Sociology, University of British Columbia, Vancouver.

Rankin, Lisa 1991 Shellfish. In *1989 and 1990 Crescent Beach Excavations, Final Report*. R.G. Matson, H. Pratt and L. Rankin, eds. Report on file, Culture Library, Ministry of Small Business, Tourism and Culture, Victoria.

Renfrew, Colin and Paul Bahn 1996 *Archaeology: Theories, Methods and Practice, 2nd Ed*. London: Thames and Hudson.

Richardson, Allan 1982 The Control of Productive Resources on the Northwest Coast of North America. In *Resource Managers: North American ands Australian Hunter Gatherers*. N.M. Williams and E.S. Hunn eds. Boulder, CO.:Westview Press. 93-112.

Robinson, S.W. and G. Thompson 1981 Radiocarbon Corrections for Marine Shell Dates with Application to Southern Pacific Northwest Coast Prehistory. *Syesis*. 14:45-57.

Sahlins, Marshall 1963 Poor Man, Rich Man, Big Man, Chief: Political Types in Melanesia and Polynesia. *Comparative Studies in Society and History* 5:285-303.

Schalk, Randall F. 1977 The Structure of an Anadromous Fish Resource. In *For Theory Building in Archaeology*. L.R. Binford ed. New York: Academic Press. 207-239.

Service, Elman 1962 *Primitive Social Organization: An Evolutionary Perspective*. New York: Random House.

Seymour, Brian 1976 1972 Salvage Excavations at DfRs 3, the Whalen Farm Site. In *Current Research Reports* R. Carlson, ed. Simon Fraser University, Department of Archaeology Publication No. 3, Burnaby. Pp 83-98.

Smith, Harlan I. 1903 Shell-heaps of the Lower Fraser river, British Columbia. *Publications of the Jesup North Pacific Expedition* 2(4), Memoirs of the American Museum of Natural History 4(4): 133-191.

Smith, Harlan I. 1907 Archaeology of the Gulf of Georgia and Puget Sound. Publications of the Jesup North Pacific Expedition 2(6). *Memoirs of the American Museum of Natural History* 4(6):303-441.

Smith, Harlan I. 1921 Unpublished Notes. BC File 55 Box 10. Ottawa: National Archives of Canada.

Smith, Harlan I. 1929 Kitchen-middens from the Pacific Coast of Canada. *National Museum of Canada Annual Report for 1927, Bulletin* 56:42-46.

Sneath, Peter and Robert Sokal 1973 *Numerical Taxonomy: The Principles and Practice of Numerical Classification.* San Francisco: W.H. Freeman and Co.

Sneed, Paul 1970 *The Archaeology of the Liquid Air Site: A Preliminary Report.* Report on File, Laboratory of Archaeology, University of British Columbia, Vancouver.

Spaulding, Albert 1955 *Prehistoric Cultural Development in the Eastern United States New Interpretations of Aboriginal American Culture History.* Anthropological Society of Washington, Pp. 12-26.

Steifel, Cheryl 1985 *The Subsistence Economy of the Locarno Beach Culture (3300-2400 B.P.).* Unpublished Master's thesis, Department of Anthropology and Sociology, University of British Columbia, Vancouver

Steward, Julian 1955 *The Theory of Culture Change: The Methodology of Multilineal Evolution.* Urbana: Illinois University Press.

Stewart, Kathlyn n.d. Fauna from the Kosapsom Site, Vancouver Island, British Columbia. Unpublished manuscript.

Stuiver, Minze and Gordon Pearson 1986 High-Precision Calibration of the Radiocarbon Time Scale, AD 1950-500 BC *Radiocarbon* 28 (2B):839-862.

Sutherland, Eileen n.d. *Report on Excavation at DgRs 11, English Bluff, Tsawwassen, 1969, DgRs 9, Tsawwassen Beach, 1970.* Report on file, Culture Library, Ministry of Small Business, Tourism and Culture, Victoria.

Suttles, Wayne 1951 *Economic Life of the Coast Salish of Haro and Rosario Straits.* Ph.D. dissertation, Department of Anthropology, University of Washington, Seattle.

Suttles, Wayne and William W. Elmendorf 1963 Linguistic Evidence for Salish Prehistory. in *Symposium on Language and Culture.* V.E. Garfield, ed. Proceedings of the 1962 Annual Spring Meeting of the American Ethnological Society, Seattle.

Taylor, R.E. 1987 *Radiocarbon Dating: An Archaeological Perspective.* Orlando: Academic Press.

Thom, Brian 1992 An Investigation of Interassemblage Variability within the Gulf of Georgia Phase. *Canadian Journal of Archaeology* 16:24-31.

Thom, Brian and R.G. Matson 1991 Whalen Farm Artifacts. In *1989 and 1990 Crescent Beach Excavations, Final Report: The Origins of the Northwest Coast Ethnographic Pattern: The Place of the Locarno Beach Phase.* R.G. Matson et al., eds. Report on file, Culture Library, Ministry of Small Business, Tourism and Culture, Victoria.

Trace, Andrew 1981 *An Examination of The Locarno Beach Phase as Represented at the Crescent Beach Site, DgRr 1, British Columbia.* Unpublished Master's thesis, Department of Archaeology, Simon Fraser University, Burnaby.

True, D.L. and R.G. Matson 1970 Cluster Analysis and Multidimensional Scaling of Archaeological Sites in Northern Chile. *Science.* 169:1201-3.

White, Leslie 1959 *The Evolution of Culture.* New York: McGraw-Hill.

Wigen, Rebecca J. 1980 *A Faunal Analysis of Two Middens on the East Coast of Vancouver Island.* Unpublished Master's thesis, Department of Anthropology, University of Victoria, Victoria.

Willey, G. and P. Phillips 1958 *Method and Theory in American Archaeology.* Chicago: University of Chicago Press.

Wilmeth, Roscoe 1978 *Canadian Archaeological Radiocarbon Dates (Revised Edition).* National Museum of Man, Mercury Series, Archaeological Survey of Canada Paper No. 77, Ottawa.

Wilson, I.R. 1988 *Archaeological Investigations at Quick's Bottom, DcRu 38.* Report on file, Culture Library, Ministry of Small Business, Tourism and Culture, Victoria.

APPENDIX 1. RADIOCARBON DATING

Radiocarbon dating is a chronometric dating procedure based on the natural decay of radioactive ^{14}C in an organism. The carbon in all living things exists in three isotopic states. The majority of carbon, 98.9% is stable ^{12}C, ^{13}C accounts for 1.1% and the remainder, about 10^{-10}% is ^{14}C (Taylor 1987). The first two isotopes are stable and the third is radioactive.

During life the ratio of ^{12}C to ^{14}C within an organism remains in equilibrium with the surrounding environment. At the time of an organism's death the uptake of new carbon ceases while ^{14}C stored within that organism continues to decay at a known rate. The ratio of ^{12}C to ^{14}C begins to change. ^{14}C has a half life of 5730 ± 40 years (Taylor 1987). By measuring the amount of 14C present in the sample the time since death can be estimated. Thus in the radiocarbon sample

$$2740 \pm 100 \text{ BP (GaK 2761)}$$

the 2740 date refers to radiocarbon years before present or BP. This actually refers to years before 1950, as that year was chosen as a standard baseline. The ± 100 refers to one standard deviation, or $\pm$ about the mean measurement of 2740 years. Thus there is a 67% chance the date lies between 2640 and 2840 BP, which is plus or minus one standard deviation about the mean. Two standard deviations about the mean provide a 95% confidence interval but raises the date range to 2540 to 2940 BP. GaK 2761 refers to the laboratory and sample number, in this case Gakushuin University, Tokyo, sample number 2761.

Radiocarbon years are not exactly equivalent to calendar years, thus one cannot simply subtract 1950 from a radiocarbon estimate to get a calendar year. A number of corrections must first be undertaken.

First, normalization corrects for isotopic fractionation. This correction deals with the ratio of ^{12}C to ^{13}C (Taylor 1987), which varies based on the diet of the organism being tested. This is affected by the type of plant consumption (C3 vs. C4 plants), and the organism's place in the food chain (primary-plants, secondary-herbivores and tertiary-carnivores) (Taylor 1987). Radiocarbon samples taken from plant material have a much smaller correction than do samples of carnivore bone.

Second, the reservoir effect is a problem associated with marine samples. In the world's oceans a large amount of dissolved stable carbon, ^{12}C, is stored and is absorbed by organism living in the sea. Much of this dissolved ^{12}C remains at the lower depths of the ocean but is periodically brought to the surface by upwelling. This produces a lower ratio of ^{14}C to ^{12}C, making them appear to be older that they actually are (Robinson and Thompson 1981). On the Northwest Coast, shell is a common source of radiocarbon samples thus this problem is an important one. The correction is thought to be -801 ± 23 years for the Gulf of Georgia but varies in other regions depending on local conditions (Robinson and Thompson 1981). This means that living marine shell will date to 801 BP. The correction for ^{13}C must also be applied to shell samples. The marine $\Delta^{13}C$ convention is to add 410 years (Robinson and Thompson 1981). Thus the overall correction for shell samples is -390 ± 23 BP.

Calibration is the final step in correlating radiocarbon years to calendar years. The rate of ^{14}C production is not constant. There are variations both in the long term based on geomagnetic variation and the short term based on heliomagnetic modulation of cosmic radiation (sunspot activity) and fossil-fuel burning (Arcas 1991b). Thus the starting ratio of 14C in an organism is dependent on when the organism lived. To calibrate radiocarbon ages one must compare the carbon sample to the calibration curve (see Figure A1.1). The calibration curve reflects the changes in ^{14}C over time. This process converts the radiocarbon age estimate to calendar years expressed as AD and BC. Calibrated years represent historical years and relate directly to dendrochronology, or tree ring dating, as a means of ascertaining age.

Returning to the GaK 2761 sample which was a shell specimen, to calibrate this sample a twofold correction is needed. The corrections for the marine reservoir effect (-801 ± 23 years) and isotopic fractionation (+410 years) yield a total correction of -390 ± 23 years. Thus 2740 ± 100 BP becomes 2350 ± 100 BP. To calibrate this date to the solar calendar, locate 2350 on the left side of Figure A1.1, Radiocarbon Years. For 95% accuracy, two standard deviations about the mean are used to give a range of 2150 to 2550 BP. These dates are shown intersecting the calibration curve at 2150 and 2750 cal BP. This means the sample GaK 2761 is related to the solar calendar years 2150 to 2750 BP or 200 to 800 BC at a confidence interval of 95%.

This example also serves to illustrate a problem with radiocarbon dating the Locarno Beach - Marpole transition. The calibration curve has a "flat spot" roughly between 2400 and 2500 BP and another between 2100 and 2200 BP. A single radiocarbon year may represent several calibrated years due to multiple intersections of the calibration curve. In this case there are not multiple intersections of the calibration curve, but there is considerable inflation of the calibrated date range related to the "flat spot". This means that there is very poor accuracy for radiocarbon dates in this range. This is unfortunate as this time period is very important in the

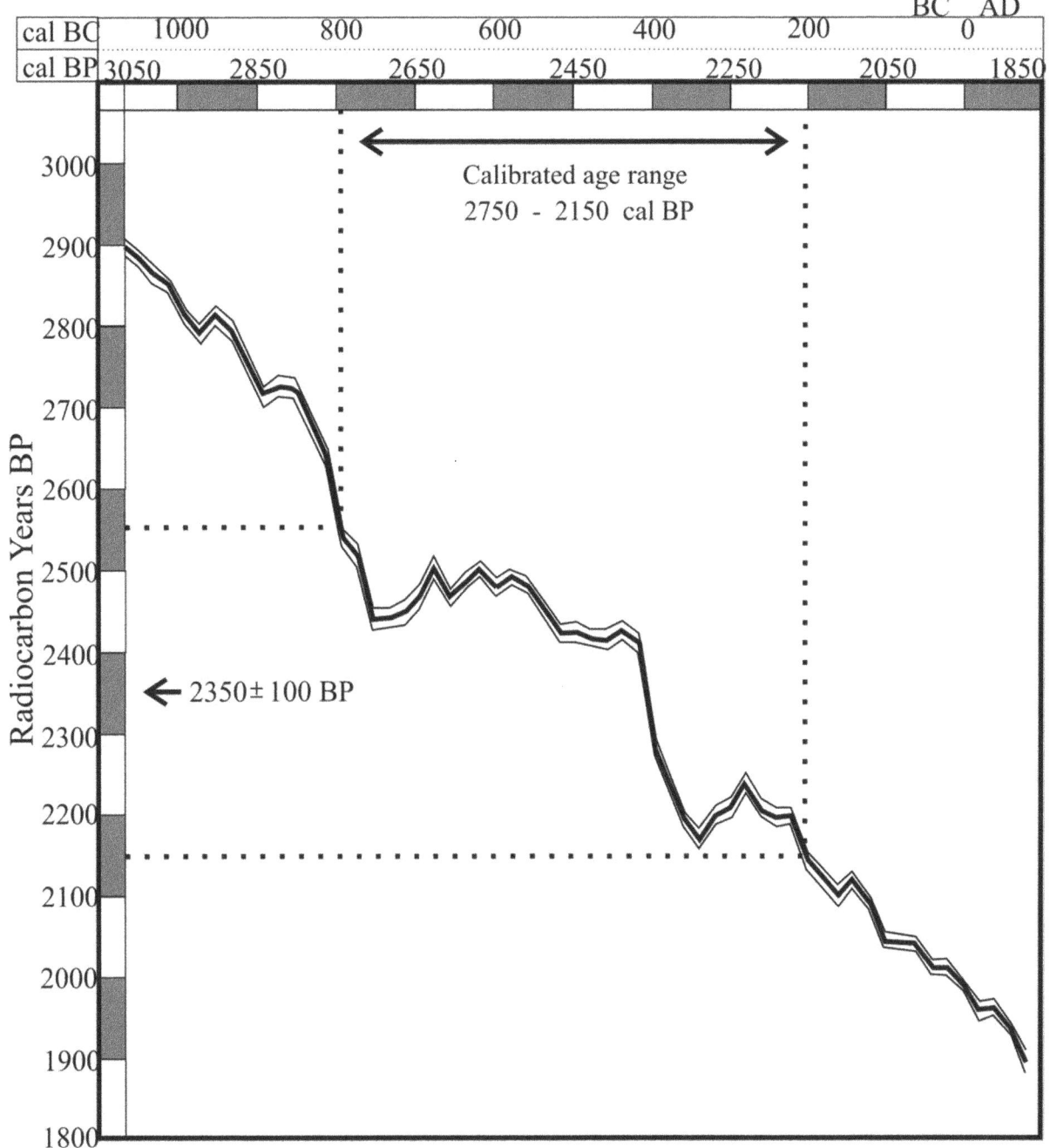

Figure A1.1 Radiocarbon Dating Calibration Curve

adapted from Stuiver and Pearson 1986:814; Pearson and Stuiver 1986:843; and Renfrew and Bahn 1996:135

development of ethnographic Northwest Coast cultures and the rise of sociocultural complexity. This "flat spot" problem is not limited to the Northwest Coast however; it is a global phenomenon with implications for prehistory in all regions.

On the Northwest Coast the most common procedure for expressing radiocarbon dates is to use raw unmodified dates, the exception being shell samples which require the two-fold correction procedure as described above.

Since there are many different means of radiocarbon calibration and available computer calibration programs raw dates are always cited. These different calibration techniques are not always comparable to each other and could cause interpretive errors if different techniques were used on different samples. By using raw dates the radiocarbon age estimates are immediately comparable to one another across the entire region.

It is important to keep in mind that the accuracy of radiocarbon dating is not precise. In this study where four clusters are found in a date range of about 1100 years, interpretations using radiocarbon dates are used sparingly. The range of each date is rarely smaller than 400 to 600 years, thus the most precise dating possible is either the relative early or late.

In this study I use raw radiocarbon age estimates with the exception of shell dates which are corrected (-390 ± 23 years). This follows general practice in Northwest Coast archaeology and is chosen to easily orient my findings within the broader field of Northwest Coast archaeology. The radiocarbon age estimates for study area components are listed in Table A1.1. A graphical depiction of their distribution can be seen in Figure 7.2.

The culture types and subphases are formal classificatory units independent of time and space (see Chapter Two). Thus inaccuracies in radiocarbon dating do not weaken their validity nor do problems in dating compromise the results of this thesis. The clusters were identified based on formal attributes. Their distribution in both geographic and chronological terms is used as an interpretive tool to explain the relationship between the clusters. The inaccuracy of radiocarbon dating for this time period means that temporal variation adds little to the interpretation.

Table A1.1 Radiocarbon Age Estimates for Selected Gulf of Georgia Site Components

Site Component	Sample Number	Age Estimate	Reference
Helen Point IIB	GaK 3200	1100 ± 90	Carlson 1970
Helen Point IIB	Gak 4936	1120 ± 100	Carlson 1970
Beach Grove 80	SFU 41	1270 ± 160	Matson et al. 1980
Helen Point IIB	Gak 4935	1370 ± 85	Carlson 1970
Beach Grove 62	UW 42	1390 ± 25	Matson et al. 1980
Beach Grove 80	SFU 42	1480 ± 80	Matson et al. 1980
Marpole II	Har 2183	1510 ± 90	Burley 1980
Beach Grove 62	UW 43	1540 ± 130	Matson et al. 1980
Garrison	GaK 4934	1580 ± 60	Burley 1980
Beach Grove 57,61,79	UW 44	1600 ± 120	Matson et al. 1980
False Narrows II	GaK 2754	1670 ± 90	Burley 1980
Point Grey	WSU 3574	1690 ± 120	Coupland 1991
Beach Grove 62	GSC 440	1730 ± 130	Matson et al. 1980
NW Cadboro Bay	RIDDL 571	1760 ± 110	Keddie 1987
Marpole II	S 93	1780 ± 60	Burley 1980
Cresent Beach III	SFU 726	1810 70	Matson et al. 1991
Cadboro Bay I	GaK 2751	1810 ± 90	Wilmeth 1978
Old Musqueam	GaK 5137	1910 80	Matson 1976
Kosapsom I	TO 5364	1960 ± 50	Mackie, pers. comm.
Point Grey	GaK 1480	1970 ± 100	Burley 1980
Point Grey	GaK 1480	1970 ± 100	Borden 1970
Glenrose Cannery III	GaK 4647	2030 ± 95	Matson 1976
Garrison	GaK 4933	2100 ± 100	Burley 1980
Marpole II	L 337	2100 ± 90	Burley 1980
Helen Point	GaK 4937	2110 ± 105	Carlson 1970
Kosapsom I	CAMS 40393	2120 ± 50	Mackie, pers. comm.

Table A1.1 Radiocarbon Age Estimates for Selected Gulf of Georgia Site Components

Site Component	Sample Number	Age Estimate	Reference
Beach Grove 57,61,79	GaK 1478	2170 ± 70	Matson et al. 1980
Point Grey	WSU 3573	2210 ± 90	Coupland 1991
Kosapsom I	CAMS 40385	2230 ± 50	Mackie, pers. comm.
Kosapsom I	CAMS 40394	2280 ± 50	Mackie, pers. comm.
Glenrose Cannery III	S 787	2300 ± 70	Matson 1976
Glenrose Cannery III	GaK 4646	2310 ± 105	Matson 1976
Kosapsom I	CAMS 40398	2320 ± 50	Mackie, pers. comm.
Glenrose Cannery III	S 790	2340 ± 120	Matson 1976
Bowker Creek	GaK 2761	2350 ± 100	Mitchell 1979, Matson n.d.
Old Musqueam	Gak 1283	2350 ± 80	Wilmeth 1969
Kosapsom I	TO 5365	2360 ± 60	Mackie, pers. comm.
DcRu 572	Beta 86772	2380 ± 60	Owens et al. 1997
Kosapsom I	CAMS 40390	2450 ± 50	Mackie, pers. comm.
Willows Beach I	GaK 5103	2490 ± 85	Curtin et al. 1991
Kosapsom I	CAMS 40386	2510 ± 50	Mackie, pers. comm.
Bowker Creek	GaK 2760	2520 ± 100	Mitchell 1979, Matson n.d.
Willows Beach I	GaK 5102	2630 ± 95	Curtin et al. 1991
Kosapsom I	CAMS 40397	2770 ± 50	Mackie, pers. comm.

Table A2.1 Artifact Frequencies

Relative Artifact Frequency for 27 Gulf of Georgia Site Components using Burley's (1980) 51 Trait Typology — page 1 of 9	Montague Harbour II	Crescent Beach III	Old Musqueam	Musqueam NE	Helen Point IIA	Helen Point IIB	Fossil Bay I	Hill Site	Glenrose Cannery III
Chipped Stone									
Flake edge tools	0.0%	40.4%	39.1%	44.2%	27.3%	18.9%	64.3%	14.1%	36.1%
Slate/Sandstone discs	2.9%	0.0%	0.0%	4.4%	2.9%	8.2%	1.8%	1.3%	0.0%
Pièces esquillées	0.0%	1.5%	5.8%	19.3%	0.0%	0.0%	0.0%	0.0%	1.7%
Microblade/core	2.9%	0.0%	0.8%	2.8%	2.2%	2.5%	0.0%	0.0%	3.3%
Chopper/chopping tools	1.0%	5.9%	0.0%	0.0%	2.2%	0.0%	0.0%	5.1%	3.9%
Corner-notch/basal-notch points	0.0%	0.0%	3.1%	1.7%	0.0%	0.0%	0.0%	0.0%	0.6%
Leaf shaped points	0.0%	0.7%	1.9%	1.1%	0.7%	2.5%	3.6%	1.3%	5.0%
Contracting stem points	2.9%	2.2%	1.9%	2.8%	1.4%	1.6%	1.8%	1.3%	1.7%
Expanding stem points	0.0%	0.0%	0.8%	0.6%	0.0%	0.0%	0.0%	0.0%	1.7%
Triangular points	4.8%	0.0%	0.4%	1.1%	5.8%	4.1%	0.0%	0.0%	0.0%
Formed bifacial cutting and/or scraping tools	0.0%	5.9%	0.4%	0.0%	1.4%	1.6%	0.0%	0.0%	3.9%
Perforators	0.0%	4.4%	0.0%	1.1%	0.0%	0.0%	0.0%	0.0%	0.6%
total chipped stone	14.3%	61.0%	54.3%	77.9%	43.9%	39.3%	71.4%	23.1%	58.3%
Ground Stone									
Triangular points	1.0%	0.0%	0.4%	0.0%	0.0%	0.8%	0.0%	0.0%	1.1%
Stemless points	0.0%	0.0%	0.4%	2.8%	0.0%	7.4%	0.0%	2.6%	1.1%
Stemmed points	1.0%	0.0%	0.0%	0.0%	0.0%	0.8%	1.8%	0.0%	0.0%
Faceted large points	0.0%	0.0%	0.0%	0.6%	0.0%	0.0%	0.0%	1.3%	0.0%
Celts/adze blades	1.0%	0.7%	2.7%	3.3%	0.0%	4.1%	1.8%	1.3%	6.7%
Decorated and decorative objects	0.0%	0.7%	0.4%	0.0%	0.0%	2.5%	0.0%	0.0%	1.1%
Labrets	0.0%	4.4%	0.0%	0.0%	0.0%	0.0%	5.4%	6.4%	2.2%
Shaped abrasive stones	3.8%	0.7%	0.0%	1.1%	9.4%	1.6%	3.6%	1.3%	0.0%
Irregular abrasive stones	19.0%	6.6%	15.1%	3.3%	38.1%	17.2%	1.8%	25.6%	16.1%
Handstones	1.0%	0.0%	0.0%	0.0%	0.0%	0.0%	0.0%	0.0%	0.0%
Stone saws	3.8%	0.0%	0.0%	0.0%	0.0%	0.0%	0.0%	7.7%	0.0%
total ground stone	30.5%	13.2%	19.0%	11.0%	47.5%	34.4%	14.3%	46.2%	28.3%

Relative Artifact Frequency for 27 Gulf of Georgia Site Components using Burley's (1980) 51 Trait Typology   page 2 of 9

	Montague Harbour II	Crescent Beach III	Old Musqueam	Musqueam NE	Helen Point IIA	Helen Point IIB	Fossil Bay I	Hill Site	Glenrose Cannery III
Pecked Stone									
Hand mauls	0.0%	0.0%	0.0%	0.0%	0.0%	0.0%	0.0%	0.0%	0.0%
Hammerstones	4.8%	6.6%	1.6%	3.9%	1.4%	0.8%	0.0%	3.8%	2.8%
Perforated stones	1.9%	0.0%	0.4%	0.6%	0.0%	0.0%	1.8%	0.0%	0.0%
Notched stones	5.7%	0.0%	0.0%	0.0%	0.7%	0.0%	0.0%	0.0%	0.0%
Mortar/bowls	0.0%	0.0%	0.4%	0.0%	0.0%	0.0%	0.0%	0.0%	0.6%
total pecked stone	12.4%	6.6%	2.3%	4.4%	2.2%	0.8%	1.8%	3.8%	3.3%
Bone									
Barbed points	1.0%	0.7%	0.0%	0.0%	0.7%	4.1%	0.0%	0.0%	0.0%
Small unipoints	3.8%	0.0%	0.4%	0.6%	0.0%	2.5%	0.0%	0.0%	0.0%
Bipoints	1.9%	1.5%	0.0%	1.1%	1.4%	2.5%	0.0%	0.0%	0.0%
Mammal bone awls	8.6%	3.7%	3.5%	1.1%	0.0%	2.5%	5.4%	6.4%	3.3%
Bird bone awls	1.0%	0.0%	7.4%	0.6%	0.0%	0.0%	0.0%	0.0%	0.0%
Needles	1.9%	0.0%	3.5%	0.0%	0.0%	0.0%	0.0%	0.0%	1.1%
Chisel/wedge tools	5.7%	3.7%	1.6%	1.7%	0.0%	0.0%	0.0%	3.8%	1.1%
Ulna awls	3.8%	0.0%	0.0%	0.6%	0.0%	0.0%	0.0%	2.6%	0.6%
Decorated or decorative objects	0.0%	0.0%	1.9%	0.6%	1.4%	0.0%	0.0%	0.0%	0.6%
Bird bone points	0.0%	0.0%	0.0%	0.0%	0.0%	0.0%	0.0%	2.6%	0.0%
Bird bone tubes	2.9%	0.7%	0.0%	0.0%	0.7%	0.8%	0.0%	1.3%	0.0%
Incisor tools	0.0%	2.9%	1.2%	0.0%	0.0%	0.0%	0.0%	3.8%	0.6%
Ground canine and other tooth pendants	1.0%	0.7%	0.8%	0.6%	0.0%	0.0%	0.0%	0.0%	0.6%
Unbarbed fixed bone point	0.0%	0.0%	1.6%	0.0%	0.0%	0.0%	0.0%	0.0%	0.0%
total bone	31.4%	14.0%	21.7%	6.6%	4.3%	12.3%	5.4%	20.5%	7.8%

Relative Artifact Frequency for 27 Gulf of Georgia Site Components using Burley's (1980) 51 Trait Typology — page 3 of 9

	Montague Harbour II	Crescent Beach III	Old Musqueam	Musqueam NE	Helen Point IIA	Helen Point IIB	Fossil Bay I	Hill Site	Glenrose Cannery III
Antler									
Composite toggling harpoon valves	0.0%	0.0%	0.0%	0.0%	0.0%	0.8%	0.0%	1.3%	0.0%
Unilaterally barbed harpoons	2.9%	0.0%	0.0%	0.0%	0.0%	0.8%	0.0%	0.0%	0.6%
Barbed points	1.9%	0.0%	0.0%	0.0%	0.7%	4.9%	1.8%	0.0%	0.6%
Wedges	2.9%	2.9%	0.8%	0.0%	1.4%	1.6%	3.6%	0.0%	1.1%
Hafts	1.9%	1.5%	0.0%	0.0%	0.0%	0.8%	0.0%	1.3%	0.0%
Pendants	0.0%	0.0%	0.0%	0.0%	0.0%	0.8%	0.0%	0.0%	0.0%
Decorated or decorative objects	0.0%	0.0%	1.2%	0.0%	0.0%	2.5%	0.0%	0.0%	0.0%
total antler	*9.5%*	*4.4%*	*1.9%*	*0.0%*	*2.2%*	*12.3%*	*5.4%*	*2.6%*	*2.2%*
Shell									
Edge tools	1.9%	0.0%	0.4%	0.0%	0.0%	0.8%	1.8%	1.3%	0.0%
Pendant/gorgets	0.0%	0.7%	0.4%	0.0%	0.0%	0.0%	0.0%	2.6%	0.0%
total shell	*1.9%*	*0.7%*	*0.8%*	*0.0%*	*0.0%*	*0.8%*	*1.8%*	*3.8%*	*0.0%*
Sample Size	105	136	258	181	139	122	56	78	180

Relative Artifact Frequency for 27 Gulf of Georgia Site Components using Burley's (1980) 51 Trait Typology — page 4 of 9

	Deep Bay II	Garrison	Whalen Farm	English Bluff	Point Grey	Marpole II	Beach Grove 80	Beach Grove 62	Beach Grove 57,61,79
Chipped Stone									
Flake edge tools	12.9%	5.2%	26.1%	9.2%	14.6%	6.6%	4.4%	7.5%	5.5%
Slate/Sandstone discs	2.9%	0.0%	1.4%	0.8%	2.2%	11.5%	0.0%	1.1%	0.3%
Pièces esquillées	0.0%	0.0%	0.0%	0.0%	0.0%	0.0%	0.0%	0.4%	0.0%
Microblade/core	0.0%	0.0%	0.0%	0.0%	0.0%	2.1%	2.9%	0.0%	0.9%
Chopper/chopping tools	2.9%	0.0%	0.0%	0.8%	2.2%	0.7%	0.0%	2.2%	1.5%
Corner-notch/basal-notch points	0.0%	0.0%	0.0%	1.5%	0.0%	1.4%	2.9%	0.0%	0.0%
Leaf shaped points	1.4%	4.1%	1.4%	1.5%	0.0%	2.1%	0.0%	2.2%	0.0%
Contracting stem points	1.4%	1.0%	0.0%	1.5%	2.2%	5.9%	0.0%	3.0%	0.6%
Expanding stem points	0.0%	0.0%	1.4%	3.8%	0.0%	2.4%	0.0%	0.7%	0.0%
Triangular points	2.9%	17.5%	1.4%	6.1%	0.0%	4.9%	1.5%	1.1%	0.0%
Formed bifacial cutting and/or scraping tools	1.4%	2.1%	5.8%	2.3%	3.4%	1.0%	1.5%	3.4%	0.0%
Perforators	0.0%	2.1%	0.0%	0.0%	0.0%	0.0%	2.9%	1.1%	0.0%
total chipped stone	*25.7%*	*32.0%*	*37.7%*	*27.5%*	*24.7%*	*38.5%*	*16.2%*	*22.8%*	*8.8%*
Ground Stone									
Triangular points	4.3%	0.0%	0.0%	0.0%	0.0%	0.0%	0.0%	0.0%	0.0%
Stemless points	4.3%	7.2%	1.4%	0.8%	0.0%	2.8%	0.0%	0.7%	0.9%
Stemmed points	1.4%	0.0%	0.0%	0.0%	0.0%	0.0%	0.0%	0.0%	0.0%
Faceted large points	0.0%	0.0%	0.0%	3.8%	0.0%	1.4%	0.0%	0.0%	0.0%
Celts/adze blades	1.4%	2.1%	1.4%	0.8%	0.0%	5.9%	2.9%	5.2%	3.0%
Decorated and decorative objects	2.9%	1.0%	1.4%	0.0%	0.0%	0.7%	0.0%	1.1%	1.5%
Labrets	0.0%	0.0%	0.0%	0.0%	0.0%	0.0%	0.0%	0.0%	0.0%
Shaped abrasive stones	1.4%	0.0%	0.0%	0.0%	2.2%	1.4%	4.4%	0.0%	2.4%
Irregular abrasive stones	15.7%	7.2%	18.8%	9.9%	12.4%	29.2%	33.8%	29.1%	15.2%
Handstones	0.0%	0.0%	0.0%	0.0%	1.1%	1.0%	0.0%	0.0%	0.0%
Stone saws	1.4%	0.0%	0.0%	0.0%	0.0%	0.3%	0.0%	0.0%	0.0%
total ground stone	*32.9%*	*17.5%*	*23.2%*	*15.3%*	*15.7%*	*42.7%*	*41.2%*	*36.2%*	*23.0%*

Relative Artifact Frequency for 27 Gulf of Georgia Site Components using Burley's (1980) 51 Trait Typology

page 5 of 9

	Deep Bay II	Garrison	Whalen Farm	English Bluff	Point Grey	Marpole II	Beach Grove 80	Beach Grove 62	Beach Grove 57,61,79
Pecked Stone									
Hand mauls	0.0%	1.0%	0.0%	0.0%	0.0%	0.3%	0.0%	0.0%	0.9%
Hammerstones	0.0%	6.2%	4.3%	2.3%	3.4%	0.7%	4.4%	3.4%	0.3%
Perforated stones	0.0%	0.0%	0.0%	0.0%	13.5%	0.3%	2.9%	0.0%	0.9%
Notched stones	0.0%	0.0%	0.0%	0.0%	0.0%	0.0%	0.0%	0.0%	0.0%
Mortar/bowls	0.0%	0.0%	2.9%	1.5%	1.1%	0.0%	0.0%	0.0%	0.0%
total pecked stone	*0.0%*	*7.2%*	*7.2%*	*3.8%*	*18.0%*	*1.4%*	*7.4%*	*3.4%*	*2.1%*
Bone									
Barbed points	0.0%	1.0%	0.0%	8.4%	0.0%	0.0%	0.0%	0.0%	0.0%
Small unipoints	4.3%	0.0%	0.0%	0.0%	3.4%	0.0%	0.0%	0.0%	1.8%
Bipoints	11.4%	0.0%	0.0%	0.0%	6.7%	0.0%	1.5%	0.0%	0.0%
Mammal bone awls	5.7%	6.2%	7.2%	7.6%	11.2%	3.8%	17.6%	6.0%	15.2%
Bird bone awls	0.0%	0.0%	2.9%	0.0%	2.2%	1.0%	1.5%	0.0%	0.9%
Needles	0.0%	1.0%	1.4%	0.0%	2.2%	1.0%	0.0%	1.5%	1.2%
Chisel/wedge tools	5.7%	5.2%	0.0%	1.5%	3.4%	1.7%	0.0%	5.2%	3.0%
Ulna awls	0.0%	11.3%	0.0%	0.8%	1.1%	0.0%	0.0%	1.1%	0.3%
Decorated or decorative objects	2.9%	2.1%	2.9%	9.2%	0.0%	0.7%	8.8%	5.2%	3.6%
Bird bone points	0.0%	0.0%	0.0%	0.0%	0.0%	0.0%	0.0%	0.4%	0.0%
Bird bone tubes	1.4%	1.0%	0.0%	3.8%	0.0%	0.7%	0.0%	2.6%	2.7%
Incisor tools	0.0%	0.0%	0.0%	3.1%	0.0%	0.0%	0.0%	0.7%	0.3%
Ground canine and other tooth pendants	0.0%	0.0%	0.0%	0.0%	1.1%	1.0%	0.0%	0.4%	0.0%
Unbarbed fixed bone point	0.0%	0.0%	0.0%	3.1%	0.0%	0.3%	0.0%	0.0%	0.0%
total bone	*31.4%*	*27.8%*	*14.5%*	*37.4%*	*31.5%*	*10.4%*	*29.4%*	*23.1%*	*29.1%*

Relative Artifact Frequency for 27 Gulf of Georgia Site Components using Burley's (1980) 51 Trait Typology

page 6 of 9

	Deep Bay II	Garrison	Whalen Farm	English Bluff	Point Grey	Marpole II	Beach Grove 80	Beach Grove 62	Beach Grove 57, 61, 79
Antler									
Composite toggling harpoon valves	5.7%	0.0%	1.4%	0.0%	0.0%	0.0%	0.0%	0.0%	1.2%
Unilaterally barbed harpoons	0.0%	3.1%	0.0%	2.3%	2.2%	0.3%	1.5%	1.1%	3.6%
Barbed points	1.4%	3.1%	4.3%	2.3%	3.4%	4.5%	0.0%	5.6%	4.8%
Wedges	2.9%	2.1%	11.6%	9.9%	4.5%	1.0%	4.4%	7.1%	18.2%
Hafts	0.0%	0.0%	0.0%	0.0%	0.0%	0.0%	0.0%	0.4%	0.0%
Pendants	0.0%	4.1%	0.0%	0.0%	0.0%	1.0%	0.0%	0.0%	0.0%
Decorated or decorative objects	0.0%	1.0%	0.0%	0.0%	0.0%	0.0%	0.0%	0.0%	0.0%
total antler	*10.0%*	*13.4%*	*17.4%*	*14.5%*	*10.1%*	*6.9%*	*5.9%*	*14.2%*	*27.9%*
Shell									
Edge tools	0.0%	1.0%	0.0%	0.0%	0.0%	0.0%	0.0%	0.4%	2.1%
Pendant/gorgets	0.0%	1.0%	0.0%	1.5%	0.0%	0.0%	0.0%	0.0%	7.0%
total shell	*0.0%*	*2.1%*	*0.0%*	*1.5%*	*0.0%*	*0.0%*	*0.0%*	*0.4%*	*9.1%*
Sample Size	70	97	69	131	89	288	68	268	330

Relative Artifact Frequency for 27 Gulf of Georgia Site Components using Burley's (1980) 51 Trait Typology — page 7 of 9

	False Narrows I	False Narrows II	NW Cadboro Bay	Willows Beach I	Bowker Creek	Cadboro Bay I	Kosapsom I	Quick's Pond	DcRu 572
Chipped Stone									
Flake edge tools	6.3%	5.4%	30.7%	24.3%	13.2%	16.6%	35.3%	42.9%	46.2%
Slate/Sandstone discs	2.3%	2.2%	0.0%	0.0%	0.0%	0.0%	0.0%	0.0%	1.9%
Pièces esquillées	1.1%	2.2%	0.0%	0.9%	2.4%	0.0%	5.9%	0.5%	0.0%
Microblade/core	1.1%	1.3%	2.0%	9.9%	28.5%	6.1%	6.4%	6.9%	5.7%
Chopper/chopping tools	1.1%	1.3%	1.0%	0.9%	0.3%	0.0%	0.0%	2.6%	2.8%
Corner-notch/basal-notch points	0.0%	0.0%	5.9%	1.1%	1.0%	1.7%	0.5%	1.6%	0.0%
Leaf shaped points	0.6%	0.0%	3.0%	2.4%	0.3%	1.7%	1.0%	3.7%	3.8%
Contracting stem points	1.1%	1.3%	4.0%	0.8%	0.3%	0.4%	1.5%	4.2%	0.9%
Expanding stem points	0.0%	0.4%	0.0%	0.1%	0.7%	0.4%	0.0%	0.0%	0.0%
Triangular points	2.8%	2.2%	2.0%	3.8%	0.0%	5.2%	0.0%	1.1%	1.9%
Formed bifacial cutting and/or scraping tools	1.7%	1.3%	17.8%	11.5%	15.6%	10.0%	1.0%	6.3%	1.9%
Perforators	1.1%	0.4%	0.0%	0.7%	0.0%	1.3%	0.0%	0.0%	1.9%
total chipped stone	19.3%	18.3%	66.3%	56.3%	62.4%	43.7%	51.5%	69.8%	67.0%
Ground Stone									
Triangular points	0.0%	0.4%	2.0%	1.6%	0.0%	0.4%	0.0%	1.1%	2.8%
Stemless points	0.6%	4.5%	2.0%	0.5%	0.0%	1.3%	0.0%	2.1%	0.9%
Stemmed points	0.6%	0.0%	2.0%	0.7%	1.4%	0.0%	1.5%	2.1%	0.9%
Faceted large points	2.3%	0.4%	1.0%	0.5%	3.7%	0.4%	0.5%	1.6%	4.7%
Celts/adze blades	2.3%	1.3%	5.9%	0.4%	0.7%	1.7%	2.0%	0.5%	3.8%
Decorated and decorative objects	2.8%	1.8%	1.0%	0.3%	0.7%	0.9%	2.5%	0.5%	5.7%
Labrets	0.0%	0.0%	0.0%	0.1%	1.4%	0.0%	0.0%	0.0%	0.0%
Shaped abrasive stones	0.6%	1.3%	2.0%	4.7%	1.7%	2.2%	2.0%	0.5%	1.9%
Irregular abrasive stones	16.5%	12.1%	1.0%	8.0%	12.9%	10.5%	4.9%	8.5%	2.8%
Handstones	1.1%	0.9%	0.0%	0.9%	0.0%	0.0%	0.0%	0.0%	0.0%
Stone saws	0.0%	0.9%	0.0%	0.3%	0.3%	0.0%	0.5%	0.0%	0.0%
total ground stone	26.7%	23.7%	16.8%	18.1%	22.7%	17.5%	13.7%	16.9%	23.6%

Relative Artifact Frequency for 27 Gulf of Georgia Site Components using Burley's (1980) 51 Trait Typology

page 8 of 9

	False Narrows I	False Narrows II	NW Cadboro Bay	Willows Beach I	Bowker Creek	Cadboro Bay I	Kosapsom I	Quick's Pond	DcRu 572
Pecked Stone									
Hand mauls	0.6%	0.0%	1.0%	0.5%	0.0%	0.0%	0.0%	0.5%	0.0%
Hammerstones	0.6%	0.4%	2.0%	0.5%	1.7%	2.6%	4.4%	12.2%	1.9%
Perforated stones	0.6%	1.8%	0.0%	0.1%	0.3%	0.0%	0.0%	0.0%	0.0%
Notched stones	0.0%	3.6%	0.0%	0.4%	0.3%	0.0%	0.0%	0.0%	0.0%
Mortar/bowls	1.1%	0.0%	0.0%	0.1%	0.3%	0.0%	0.0%	0.0%	0.0%
total pecked stone	*2.8%*	*5.8%*	*3.0%*	*1.7%*	*2.7%*	*2.6%*	*4.4%*	*12.7%*	*1.9%*
Bone									
Barbed points	2.8%	0.0%	0.0%	0.5%	0.0%	1.3%	0.5%	0.0%	0.0%
Small unipoints	1.1%	2.2%	1.0%	2.5%	1.4%	3.9%	6.4%	0.0%	0.0%
Bipoints	0.0%	0.4%	0.0%	2.0%	0.0%	2.2%	1.0%	0.0%	0.0%
Mammal bone awls	17.0%	11.6%	4.0%	3.7%	3.1%	4.8%	5.9%	0.0%	2.8%
Bird bone awls	1.1%	1.3%	0.0%	0.3%	0.0%	0.4%	0.0%	0.0%	0.0%
Needles	6.3%	0.9%	1.0%	0.5%	1.4%	0.9%	0.0%	0.0%	0.0%
Chisel/wedge tools	0.6%	2.2%	0.0%	0.1%	0.0%	0.9%	0.5%	0.0%	0.0%
Ulna awls	1.1%	0.9%	0.0%	0.9%	0.3%	2.6%	0.0%	0.0%	0.0%
Decorated or decorative objects	1.1%	0.9%	0.0%	0.5%	0.0%	0.9%	0.0%	0.5%	1.9%
Bird bone points	0.0%	2.7%	0.0%	0.3%	0.0%	0.0%	2.5%	0.0%	0.0%
Bird bone tubes	1.7%	2.7%	0.0%	0.4%	0.0%	1.3%	0.0%	0.0%	0.0%
Incisor tools	0.0%	0.0%	0.0%	0.0%	0.0%	0.4%	0.5%	0.0%	0.0%
Ground canine and other tooth pendants	1.1%	0.9%	1.0%	0.4%	0.0%	0.0%	0.0%	0.0%	0.0%
Unbarbed fixed bone point	0.6%	3.1%	1.0%	1.3%	0.0%	1.3%	1.0%	0.0%	0.0%
total bone	*34.7%*	*29.9%*	*7.9%*	*13.5%*	*6.1%*	*21.0%*	*18.1%*	*0.5%*	*4.7%*

Relative Artifact Frequency for 27 Gulf of Georgia Site Components using Burley's (1980) 51 Trait Typology — page 9 of 9

	False Narrows I	False Narrows II	NW Cadboro Bay	Willows Beach I	Bowker Creek	Cadboro Bay I	Kosapsom I	Quick's Pond	DcRu 572
Antler									
Composite toggling harpoon valves	0.6%	0.9%	0.0%	1.2%	0.0%	1.7%	0.0%	0.0%	0.0%
Unilaterally barbed harpoons	1.7%	0.4%	3.0%	0.5%	0.3%	6.6%	1.5%	0.0%	1.9%
Barbed points	8.0%	5.8%	0.0%	0.0%	0.0%	0.0%	0.0%	0.0%	0.0%
Wedges	2.3%	4.5%	1.0%	6.1%	1.4%	2.6%	1.0%	0.0%	0.0%
Hafts	0.0%	0.9%	0.0%	0.7%	0.3%	0.4%	0.0%	0.0%	0.0%
Pendants	1.7%	3.6%	0.0%	0.0%	0.0%	0.4%	0.0%	0.0%	0.9%
Decorated or decorative objects	0.6%	0.4%	0.0%	0.1%	0.0%	0.4%	0.0%	0.0%	0.0%
total antler	*14.8%*	*16.5%*	*4.0%*	*8.6%*	*2.0%*	*12.2%*	*2.5%*	*0.0%*	*2.8%*
Shell									
Edge tools	0.6%	2.7%	2.0%	0.4%	4.1%	3.1%	5.4%	0.0%	0.0%
Pendant/gorgets	1.1%	3.1%	0.0%	1.5%	0.0%	0.0%	4.4%	0.0%	0.0%
total shell	*1.7%*	*5.8%*	*2.0%*	*1.8%*	*4.1%*	*3.1%*	*9.8%*	*0.0%*	*0.0%*
Sample Size	176	224	101	758	295	229	204	189	106

Table A3.1 Metric Multidimensional Scaling Distance Matrix

	Montague Harbour II	Crescent Beach III	Old Musqueam	Musqueam NE	Helen Point IIA	Helen Point IIB	Fossil Bay I	Hill Site	Glenrose Cannery III	Deep Bay II	Garrison	Whalen Farm	English Bluff	Point Grey
Montague Harbour II	0													
Crescent Beach III	0.0269	0												
Old Musqueam	0.0267	0.0152	0											
Musqueam NE	0.0301	0.0164	0.0146	0										
Helen Point IIA	0.0226	0.021	0.0196	0.0226	0									
Helen Point IIB	0.0204	0.0233	0.0200	0.0223	0.0171	0								
Fossil Bay I	0.0296	0.0167	0.0190	0.0176	0.0240	0.0245	0							
Hill Site	0.0199	0.0193	0.0227	0.0259	0.0201	0.0208	0.0257	0						
Glenrose Cannery III	0.0254	0.0125	0.0106	0.0157	0.0176	0.0173	0.0187	0.0197	0					
Deep Bay II	0.0186	0.0233	0.0226	0.0265	0.0207	0.0149	0.0261	0.0180	0.0207	0				
Garrison	0.0216	0.0247	0.0270	0.0292	0.0283	0.0214	0.0299	0.0242	0.0251	0.0222	0			
Whalen Farm	0.0229	0.0189	0.0161	0.0222	0.0176	0.0170	0.0223	0.0196	0.0146	0.0184	0.0235	0		
English Bluff	0.0228	0.0242	0.0229	0.0277	0.0249	0.0208	0.0285	0.0227	0.0219	0.0209	0.0199	0.0173	0	
Point Grey	0.0174	0.0214	0.0223	0.0265	0.0229	0.0203	0.0256	0.0208	0.0209	0.0166	0.0243	0.0176	0.0208	0
Marpole II	0.0198	0.0279	0.0221	0.0253	0.0177	0.0147	0.0297	0.0194	0.0198	0.0201	0.0229	0.0201	0.0205	0.0227
Beach Grove 80	0.0198	0.0273	0.0253	0.0291	0.0179	0.0230	0.0293	0.0218	0.0236	0.0234	0.0243	0.0198	0.0210	0.0208
Beach Grove 62	0.0184	0.0229	0.0219	0.0278	0.0194	0.0193	0.0285	0.0162	0.0178	0.0177	0.0195	0.0146	0.0152	0.0182
Beach Grove 57,61,79	0.0193	0.0281	0.0245	0.0308	0.0270	0.0220	0.0291	0.0222	0.0243	0.0201	0.0226	0.0178	0.0180	0.0186
False Narrows I	0.0183	0.0267	0.0220	0.0286	0.0238	0.0170	0.0294	0.0224	0.0220	0.0189	0.0206	0.0191	0.0188	0.0177
False Narrows II	0.0163	0.0262	0.0238	0.0275	0.0259	0.0186	0.0285	0.0206	0.0239	0.0179	0.0201	0.0208	0.0193	0.0170
NW Cadboro Bay	0.0281	0.0191	0.0182	0.0203	0.0230	0.0208	0.0201	0.0269	0.0151	0.0249	0.0266	0.0205	0.0253	0.0249
Willows Beach I	0.0234	0.0181	0.0197	0.0223	0.0187	0.0177	0.0228	0.0243	0.0172	0.0208	0.0254	0.0175	0.0216	0.0207
Bowker Creek	0.0264	0.0242	0.0230	0.0276	0.0252	0.0226	0.0285	0.0240	0.0204	0.0241	0.0292	0.0227	0.0264	0.0229
Cadboro Bay I	0.0195	0.0206	0.0204	0.0238	0.0212	0.0210	0.0259	0.0211	0.0183	0.0183	0.0200	0.0182	0.0185	0.0187
Kosapsom I	0.0258	0.0159	0.0151	0.0157	0.0222	0.0210	0.0184	0.0228	0.0158	0.0232	0.0267	0.0207	0.0253	0.0233
Quick's Pond	0.0298	0.0128	0.0161	0.0153	0.0206	0.0224	0.0184	0.0250	0.0127	0.0250	0.0271	0.0195	0.0270	0.0255
DcRu 572	0.0303	0.0162	0.0170	0.0135	0.0211	0.0202	0.0149	0.0263	0.0137	0.0230	0.0267	0.0213	0.0260	0.0263

Table A3.1 Metric Multidimensional Scaling Distance Matrix

	Marpole II	Beach Grove 80	Beach Grove 62	Beach Grove 57,61,79	False Narrows I	False Narrows II	NW Cadboro Bay	Willows Beach I	Bowker Creek	Cadboro Bay I	Kosapsom I	Quick's Pond	DcRu 572
Marpole II	0												
Beach Grove 80	0.0185	0											
Beach Grove 62	0.0128	0.0147	0										
Beach Grove 57,61,79	0.0215	0.0185	0.0161	0									
False Narrows I	0.0170	0.0181	0.0167	0.0144	0								
False Narrows II	0.0186	0.0215	0.0180	0.0140	0.0125	0							
NW Cadboro Bay	0.0234	0.0287	0.0251	0.0278	0.0264	0.0268	0						
Willows Beach I	0.0237	0.0244	0.0231	0.0243	0.0223	0.0209	0.0151	0					
Bowker Creek	0.0249	0.0269	0.0251	0.0261	0.0242	0.0241	0.0199	0.0162	0				
Cadboro Bay I	0.0216	0.0227	0.0208	0.0217	0.0202	0.0195	0.0168	0.0111	0.0165	0			
Kosapsom I	0.0278	0.0267	0.0265	0.0254	0.0253	0.0228	0.0169	0.0169	0.0212	0.0173	0		
Quick's Pond	0.0257	0.0285	0.0259	0.0310	0.0282	0.0288	0.0154	0.0165	0.0220	0.0198	0.0160	0	
DcRu 572	0.0259	0.0271	0.0257	0.0290	0.0251	0.0277	0.0155	0.0190	0.0246	0.0209	0.0154	0.0117	0

Metric Multidimensional Scaling Factor Matrix

Site Components	Dimensions							
	1	2	3	4	5	6	7	8
Montague Harbour II	-0.0117	-0.0010	-0.0002	-0.0054	0.0063	-0.0003	-0.0049	0.0024
Crescent Beach III	0.0103	0.0016	-0.0051	-0.0039	0.0020	-0.0057	0.0040	0.0004
Old Musqueam	0.0077	0.0031	-0.0014	0.0002	-0.0048	0.0040	0.0030	0.0016
Musqueam Northeast	0.0134	0.0048	-0.0034	0.0015	0.0011	0.0049	-0.0012	0.0034
Helen Point IIA	0.0016	0.0089	0.0093	-0.0024	0.0019	-0.0019	-0.0045	-0.0022
Helen Point IIB	-0.0021	0.0000	0.0037	0.0039	0.0048	0.0064	-0.0011	-0.0045
Fossil Bay II	0.0127	0.0037	-0.0075	-0.0038	-0.0004	0.0010	-0.0048	-0.0021
Hill Site	-0.0043	0.0051	0.0001	-0.0075	0.0054	-0.0018	0.0074	0.0038
Glenrose Cannery III	0.0073	0.0030	0.0013	0.0009	-0.0021	0.0004	0.0044	0.0005
Deep Bay II	-0.0055	-0.0004	-0.0003	-0.0029	0.0060	0.0036	0.0021	-0.0079
Garrison	-0.0075	-0.0027	-0.0080	0.0095	0.0078	-0.0057	0.0001	0.0024
Whalen Farm	-0.0007	0.0027	0.0001	-0.0001	-0.0058	-0.0020	0.0026	-0.0055
English Bluff	-0.0075	-0.0007	-0.0040	0.0061	-0.0042	-0.0048	0.0029	-0.0031
Point Grey	-0.0060	-0.0023	-0.0025	-0.0077	-0.0012	0.0000	-0.0001	-0.0042
Marpole II	-0.0078	0.0062	0.0074	0.0060	0.0018	0.0047	0.0015	0.0030

	Dimensions							
Site Components	1	2	3	4	5	6	7	8
Beach Grove 80	-0.0097	0.0069	0.0032	-0.0010	-0.0049	-0.0055	-0.0075	0.0037
Beach Grove 62	-0.0095	0.0059	0.0009	0.0019	-0.0018	-0.0038	0.0045	0.0001
Beach Grove 57,61,79	-0.0124	-0.0019	-0.0054	-0.0012	-0.0076	0.0018	-0.0006	0.0001
False Narrows I	-0.0105	-0.0013	-0.0013	0.0025	-0.0033	0.0053	-0.0019	0.0010
False Narrows II	-0.0106	-0.0046	-0.0044	-0.0012	0.0002	0.0058	-0.0010	0.0029
Northwest Cadboro Bay	0.0101	-0.0056	0.0034	0.0048	-0.0010	-0.0004	-0.0004	0.0000
Willows Beach I	0.0044	-0.0080	0.0049	-0.0004	-0.0007	-0.0027	-0.0030	-0.0028
Bowker Creek	0.0023	-0.0114	0.0093	-0.0037	-0.0029	-0.0001	0.0040	0.0039
Cadboro Bay I	-0.0004	-0.0090	0.0030	0.0013	0.0025	-0.0032	-0.0007	-0.0004
Kosapsom I	0.0097	-0.0043	-0.0032	-0.0034	-0.0003	0.0017	-0.0024	0.0041
Quick's Pond	0.0140	0.0000	0.0017	0.0018	0.0012	-0.0031	0.0011	0.0003
DcRu 572	0.0128	0.0014	-0.0017	0.0044	0.0002	0.0015	-0.0034	-0.0013

Percent of variance explained by dimension							
1	2	3	4	5	6	7	8
33.49%	10.59%	8.79%	7.33%	6.40%	5.81%	5.14%	4.28%

Total variance accounted for	81%

www.ingramcontent.com/pod-product-compliance
Lightning Source LLC
Chambersburg PA
CBHW061547010526
44114CB00027B/2958